SUSANNE & ARNE SALIG

# THE
# SELF-COMPETENCE
# BLUEPRINT

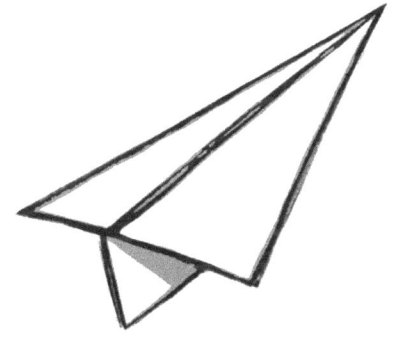

**MELLENBURG**

First edition: June 2025
Published by Mellenburg Publishing
ISBN 979-8-89965-038-3

Interior design by Qlos Q.
This book is intended for educational and informational purposes only.
It does not constitute psychological or medical advice.
Always consult a qualifi ed professional
regarding health-related decisions.

**www.self-competence.com**

"

*You have a right to be exactly who you are.*

— **Michelle Obama**

# Table of Contents

# The House of Self-Competence

## Why This Book?

Imagine you are the architect of your own life. You have blueprints, materials, and the desire to create something stable and beautiful—your very own life house. But sometimes things don't go according to plan. Perhaps you've built on sandy ground without realizing it. Or the walls are thin because you lacked important building materials. Maybe you tried to erect a magnificent roof before the foundation had properly set.

This is exactly where this book comes in. It shows you, through a simple yet powerful metaphor, how to build a stable "House of Self-Competence"—stone by stone, level by level.

We—Susanne and Arne Salig—worked for years in the psychological services of various clinics. In our daily work with people in crisis and transition, we gained a fundamental insight: The most effective changes always begin with the "self." Together with psychologist Melanie Theissler, our self-competence model was born.

Between therapy sessions, group offerings, and the often hectic clinic routine, we had only limited time for each patient. This limitation became our greatest advantage—it forced us to search for the most effective impulses. We looked for methods and exercises that would work not only in the protected space of the clinic but would also endure in real life. We sought approaches that would have a lasting effect and empower people to take charge of their own lives.

## How This Model Emerged

It was an ordinary Tuesday afternoon in the clinic when we were discussing our experiences during a short break. "Have you noticed," Susanne asked, "that the issue of self-esteem plays a role for almost all patients?" Arne nodded: "Absolutely. But somehow, just working on that is never enough."

That was the beginning of an intensive exploration of the various "self" concepts so frequently used in psychology: self-esteem, self-love, self-awareness, self-empowerment—how are these actually connected? Is there a hierarchy, a structure? And why do so many well-intentioned approaches that directly target self-esteem fail?

We began to systematically observe, document, and discuss. Each patient, each therapy session, each group work became a small mosaic piece in a larger picture. Slowly, from practical work with over 1,000 patients—in collaboration with psychologist Melanie Theissler—a model emerged that we now call the "House of Self-Competence."

What began as theoretical reflection became a practical guide for our daily work. And the amazing thing was: it worked. Not just for individual patients, but as a universal principle.

## What We Discovered

Perhaps the most important insight was this: You cannot work on self-esteem alone. It's like trying to build a roof without first erecting the foundation and walls—an endeavor doomed to fail.

"Love yourself!" or "You need to work on your self-esteem!"—such well-intentioned advice is about as helpful as telling someone with depression to "Just be happy!" What's missing is the how, the structure, the path to get there.

Here are our key insights in brief:

1. **Without self-awareness, nothing works.** You cannot value what you don't perceive. The honest assessment of your needs, strengths, weaknesses, and goals is the foundation for everything else.

2. **Awareness alone is not enough—acceptance is the next step.** This doesn't mean resignation, but accepting the current state as a starting point for change. This includes making peace with your own history. Hope for a better past is futile—but shaping a better future lies in your hands.

3. **Self-empowerment is the game-changer.** The realization that you have influence over your life and the willingness to stand by your decisions is a supporting pillar of the house.

4. **Self-care is not a luxury, but a necessity.** It stabilizes the entire structure and ensures that it can withstand storms.

5. **Self-esteem is like a protective roof.** It doesn't emerge through positive affirmations, but as a natural consequence of the elements underneath.

In our clinical work, something else became clear: People with significant psychological burdens ALWAYS show deficits in at least one, but usually in several areas of self-competence. This is not a judgment, but an important diagnostic insight—and at the same time a glimmer of hope. Because when we understand which elements of the house need special attention, we can target them specifically.

## The House Model—An Overview

Our "House of Self-Competence" consists of five main elements that stand in a clear hierarchical relationship to each other:

## The Foundation: Self-Awareness

The basis for everything. This is about recognizing and acknowledging your own needs, goals, strengths, and weaknesses.

## The Supporting Walls:

- **Self-Acceptance (with Self-Forgiveness)** — a wall dedicated to accepting your current state and making peace with your own history.

- **Self-Empowerment (with Self-Efficacy)** — the second supporting wall, dedicated to actively shaping your own life and the awareness of your own ability to act.

## The Stabilizing Support: Self-Care

It ensures that the house doesn't wobble with every storm and that the substance doesn't gradually decay.

## The Protective Roof: Self-Esteem

With its three aspects:

- Self-Love (directed inward)
- Self-Assurance (directed outward)
- Self-Confidence (effective both inward and outward)

As with any house, the order of construction is crucial. No one would think of building the roof first and then pouring the foundation. The same applies to self-competence. Each element builds upon the previous one and cannot exist stably without it.

### Definition of Self-Competence (according to Salig/Theissler):

"Self-competence is the ability to consciously perceive, reflect upon, and responsibly direct one's own thoughts, feelings, and actions, to accept oneself with one's entire personality, and to utilize individual potentials."

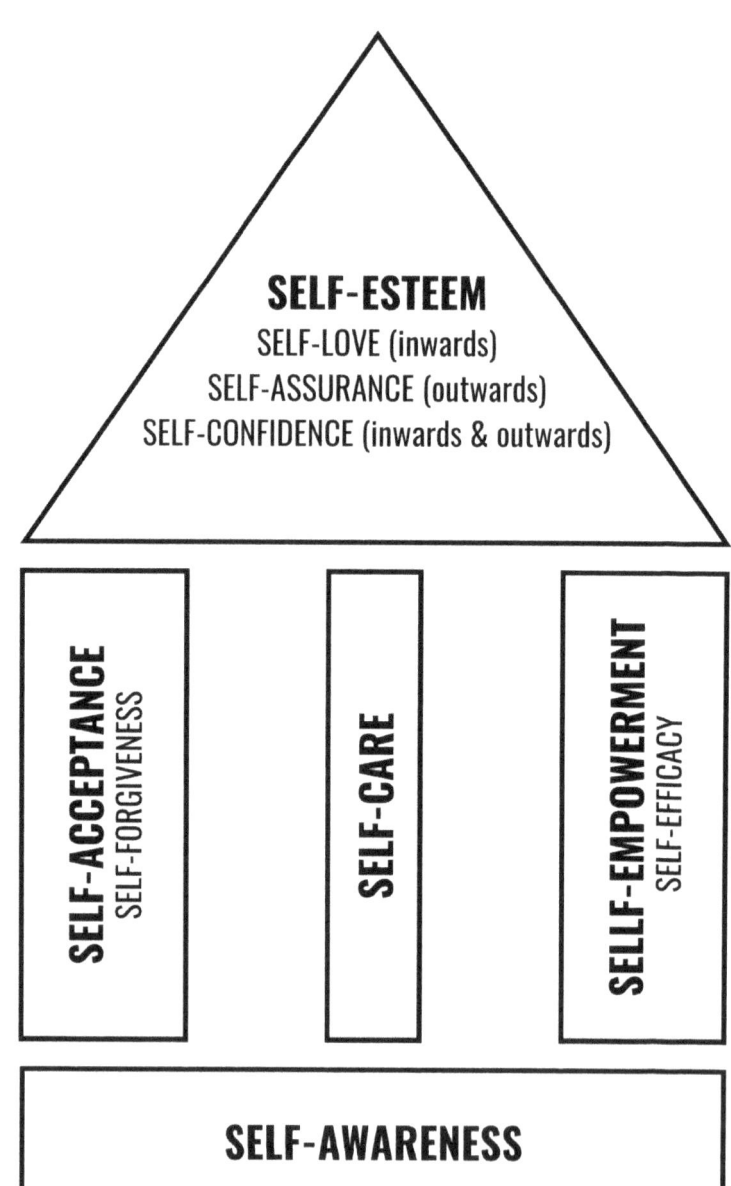

## Who Is This Book For?

This book is for you if...

- you feel like you're not progressing in life, even though you're doing everything "right"

- you suffer from a lack of self-esteem but don't know how to change it

- you often feel overwhelmed, exhausted, or burned out

- you notice that you keep falling into the same relationship patterns

- you want to find your way back to life after an illness-related break

- you're facing major changes professionally or personally

- you feel like you're not living the life you really want to live

- you're a therapist, coach, or counselor looking for a practice-proven model that you can use in your work

In short: This book is for anyone who wants to place their "House of Self-Competence" on a stable foundation—whether as a new build, renovation, or rebuilding after a personal storm.

## How to Use This Book

You're not holding a theoretical textbook in your hands, but a practical blueprint for your personal House of Self-Competence. Each chapter is structured so that you first understand the respective element in its significance, then learn about typical obstacles and supportive factors, and finally receive concrete exercises to work with.

Here are some suggestions for how you can work with this book:

- **Read it from front to back** if you want a systematic overview.

- **Start with the chapter that appeals to you most** if you already have an idea where your "house" needs special attention.

- **Use the book as a reference** that you can return to again and again.

- **Do the exercises!** Self-competence is not a theoretical discipline, but a practical skill that grows through practice.

- **Be patient with yourself.** Rome wasn't built in a day, and neither will be your House of Self-Competence.

In the following chapters, we will look at each element of the house in more detail, explain its significance, and show you how to strengthen it. We will repeatedly return to the house metaphor to illustrate the connections.

Before we dive deeper, we'd like to give you a question to consider: When you look at your personal House of Self-Competence—which part do you think needs the most attention? This intuitive assessment can help you to be particularly attentive when we discuss the corresponding element.

We invite you to take a short test of your self-competence:

(https://www.selbstkompetenz.org.en.test)

Now, let's begin—let's lay the foundation together for your stable House of Self-Competence!

CHAPTER 1

# The Foundation - Self-Awareness

---

*"I don't feel myself anymore."*
*"I feel like I'm just functioning."*
*"I'm not really living - I'm being lived."*

— Statements from our patients

---

## Self-Check: How's Your Self-Awareness?

Before we dive deeper, take a moment for an honest self-assessment. The following five characteristics indicate good self-awareness. How many apply to you?

- You know your psychological and physical needs
- You know yourself with your strengths and weaknesses
- You know how you affect others
- You know your dreams, wishes, and goals
- You know what defines you as a personality

The more questions you can answer with a clear "Yes," the more stable your foundation already is. But don't worry if you're uncertain about some or even all of these points—that's exactly what this chapter is for.

## What Does Self-Awareness Really Mean?

Imagine driving through a foggy landscape. The road ahead is only faintly visible, signposts blur in the gray. Lights occasionally appear, then disappear again. You drive more slowly, with more effort, more uncertain. The feeling of not knowing exactly where you are and where you actually want to go spreads.

This is exactly what a life with limited self-awareness feels like.

When we talk about self-awareness, we don't just mean noticing when you're hungry or when your foot falls asleep. These basic physical perceptions are important, but self-awareness goes far beyond that. It's about the deep, honest inventory of your entire inner world:

- Who am I really?
- What defines me?
- What are my strengths and weaknesses?
- What emotions move me?
- What do I need to feel good?
- What do I dream of?
- Where do I want to go in my life?
- What gives my existence meaning?

These questions sound big and philosophical—and they are. But they are also entirely practical and relevant to everyday life. Because only when you are clear about these things can you lead a life that suits you.

## The Lost Access to Self

"I don't even know anymore what I like." This sentence falls alarmingly often in our therapy conversations. People who have functioned for years—for their job, family, partner, society—have lost access to themselves. They have stopped asking what THEY want, and instead have only paid attention to what others expect of them.

Do you know this feeling? Those moments when you wonder how you ended up in this life situation? When you feel like your life doesn't really belong to you? When you realize that you get up in the morning to do a job that doesn't fulfill you, living in a relationship that drains you, living in an environment that doesn't suit you?

These are classic signs that self-awareness has been lost—and with it, the compass that could show you which path is right for you.

## The Negative Filter

Another phenomenon we observe again and again: The view of oneself is often negatively colored. When asked "What do you like about yourself?" many people hesitate. The question "What don't you like about yourself?" quickly brings forth a long list.

This negative filter is like glasses that distort everything. You perceive your weaknesses as oversized and in garish colors, while your strengths appear blurry and pale. This distorted self-awareness leads to an unstable foundation—and thus to a shaky House of Self-Competence.

### The Core of Your Personality

With good self-awareness, you get to know the core of your personality—what defines you, regardless of the roles you take on in life. This core is like the floor plan of your house—it provides the structure upon which everything else is built.

In the stress of everyday life, we often live more or less far away from this personality core. The further we distance ourselves, the more we feel like we're just "functioning." The closer we are to ourselves, the more authentically we can live.

It becomes problematic when functioning becomes such a habit that we can no longer perceive our personality core. When we can no longer describe what actually defines us, what's important to us, what excites us. Then the foundation of our House of Self-Competence is so buried that we must first uncover it again.

The good news: Self-awareness can be trained. With the right methods, you can rediscover access to yourself—and thus take the first and most important step in building your House of Self-Competence.

## Why a Strong Foundation Is Crucial

Imagine trying to build a house on swampy ground. You can erect the most beautiful walls, put on an artistic roof—without a stable foundation, the house will sink into the ground at the first sign of stress.

The same applies to self-competence. Self-awareness is the foundation upon which everything else rests. Without it, all other efforts will sooner or later fail.

## The View from the Roof

Let's consider the matter from the roof of the house—the self-esteem:

- How can you value something that you don't perceive (or only perceive in a distorted way)?
- How can you accept something if you don't know what?
- How can you take responsibility if you don't know exactly what for?
- And how can you take good care of yourself if you don't know what's good for you?

These questions make it crystal clear why self-awareness is so fundamental. It is the starting point for everything else. Without a clear picture of yourself, your life resembles a journey without a map—you know neither where you are nor where you want to go.

## Life Without a Compass

Without good self-awareness, you are steered by everyday life and the needs of other people. You have no chance to counter-steer because you don't know in which direction. You may sense that something isn't right, but you can't name what it is or what you would need instead.

This leads to a feeling of disorientation and powerlessness. You feel at the mercy of circumstances, as if you were a passenger in your own life rather than the driver. This passivity prevents you from actively setting the course for a fulfilled life.

## Self-Awareness as a Prerequisite for Change

"What I don't perceive, I cannot change." This simple sentence summarizes why self-awareness is the starting point for any personal development.

An example: Perhaps you notice that you are often exhausted and have no energy left. Without good self-awareness, you might think: "I'm just weak" or "That's just how life is." With good self-awareness, you might realize that you constantly feel responsible for everyone, can't set boundaries, and ignore your own needs. This realization is the first step towards change.

Or another example: You feel dissatisfied in your job, but don't know why—after all, you earn well and have nice colleagues. With sharpened self-awareness, you might recognize that you're missing the creative aspect, that you've chosen a profession that meets your parents' expectations but not your own talents and interests.

Without these insights, you grope in the dark. You sense that something is wrong, but you can't name it and therefore can't change it.

## Renewing the Foundation

In our house model, self-awareness is the foundation, and as with a real house, the foundation should be checked regularly and repaired if necessary. Even if you've already built an entire "House of Self-Competence," it's worth regularly returning to self-awareness and seeing if anything has changed.

People develop, circumstances change, and what was true yesterday may no longer be fitting today. A lifelong practice in self-awareness ensures that you can keep pace with these changes and continually realign your life to your current needs.

## Obstacles on the Path to Self-Awareness

The path to healthy self-awareness is not always easy. There are numerous obstacles that can block our clear view of ourselves. Some of these obstacles are deeply rooted in our childhood, others arise from social influences or current life circumstances.

### The Imprint of Childhood

The foundations for our self-awareness are laid in our early years. The social environment, especially the upbringing by our parents or other important caregivers, plays a decisive role.

Imagine a small child just discovering the world. They're excited by a colorful butterfly and run after it. The parents' reaction to this natural behavior shapes how the child perceives themselves:

- "Look how beautiful the butterfly is! What excites you about it?" – This reaction reinforces the child's perception and curiosity.
- "Leave the butterfly alone, you'll break it!" – This reaction conveys to the child that their natural impulses are problematic.
- "Stop running around, people don't do that!" – This reaction teaches the child to suppress their own impulses.

Over the years, such reactions shape the way we perceive and evaluate ourselves.

## The Authoritarian Parenting Style

Particularly formative is an authoritarian parenting style, in which the child is clearly told what is "right" and what is "wrong." In this environment, the child does not learn to trust their own perception, but orients themselves according to external guidelines.

The child might think: "I find the picture I painted beautiful, but Dad says it's not good. So it must be bad." Over time, they lose confidence in their own perception and instead adopt the evaluations of others.

## The Effects of Criticism

Frequent criticism of the behavior—or even more harmful—of the person of the child can permanently distort self-awareness. If a child constantly hears that they are "too loud," "too slow," "too dreamy," or generally "not good enough," they will internalize these evaluations.

These internalized critical voices often accompany us into adulthood and influence how we perceive ourselves. They become an inner critic who constantly evaluates us and is usually too harsh.

## The Power of Comparisons

Another major obstacle to healthy self-awareness is constant comparison with others. This "measuring up" begins in childhood: Who is faster, stronger, more popular, smarter?

In adulthood, these comparisons continue: Who has the better job, the nicer house, the happier relationship, the more successful children? These comparisons almost always lead to a distorted self-awareness, usually in the sense of devaluing oneself.

## The Social Media Effect

In our current time, this problem has been dramatically intensified by social media. We are constantly confronted with perfectly staged excerpts from the lives of others. These images are made for external consumption—they don't show reality, but an idealized version of it.

The focus shifts more and more away from one's own needs and towards the question: "How do I please others?" The result is increasing inauthenticity, where we no longer feel ourselves, but just function and perform.

## Putting Aside One's Own Needs

Another common obstacle to healthy self-awareness is the chronic setting aside of one's own needs. Especially women (but not only them) are often told that their own needs are less important than those of others—the partner, the children, the parents, the colleagues.

This constant setting aside leads to one's own needs eventually no longer being perceived at all. A life emerges that is primarily oriented towards the needs of others, while one's own person increasingly recedes into the background. The result: You lose yourself—in work, in relationships, in the role as a parent.

## The Fear of What We Might Find

Sometimes it's also the fear of what we might find in an honest self-examination that prevents us from having a healthy self-awareness. Perhaps we fear discovering that we're on the wrong path, that our relationship isn't working, that our job makes us unhappy.

This fear can be so great that we prefer to remain in the fog rather than face the clarity that true self-awareness would bring. But as with any fear: Avoidance only strengthens it, while looking at it reduces it in the long run.

## Factors That Promote Deeper Self-Awareness

As numerous as the obstacles may be—there are just as many factors that can promote healthy self-awareness. With the right conditions and practices, everyone can learn to perceive themselves more clearly and benevolently.

### Conscious Experience of the Here and Now

An important basis for deeper self-awareness is the conscious perception of the present moment. When you consciously experience your life with all your senses, you create a kind of continuous present in which you can encounter yourself.

This doesn't mean that you should constantly live in meditative immersion. Rather, it's about pausing briefly again and again and perceiving:

- How does my body feel right now?
- What thoughts are going through my head?
- What feelings are present?
- What am I perceiving with my senses?

These moments of conscious experience are like small windows to yourself. The more often you open them, the better you get to know yourself.

## Regular Pausing

In addition to conscious experience in everyday life, targeted, regular pausing is conducive to deeper self-awareness. Take a moment several times a day to check in with yourself:

- What am I feeling right now?
- Am I currently with myself or outside of myself?
- Am I currently going MY way or the way others have planned for me?
- Am I currently doing something that's good for me or something that exhausts me?

These small check-ins help you not to lose contact with yourself and to counter-steer in time when you notice that you're going off course.

## Reflection and Self-Exploration

Deeper self-awareness also emerges through conscious reflection and self-exploration. This can happen in the form of a journal, through conversations with trusted people, or through targeted exercises.

This is not about superficial self-optimization, but about an honest exploration of what defines you:

- What touched or moved me today?
- In which moments did I feel alive?
- What stressed or burdened me?
- Which of my needs were met, which were not?

This reflection helps you to recognize patterns and develop a deeper understanding of yourself.

## A Supportive Environment

Another important factor for healthy self-awareness is a supportive social environment. People who accept you as you are, who give you honest but benevolent feedback, and who encourage you to go your own way.

In such an environment, you can feel safe to show yourself as you really are, without fear of rejection or criticism. This creates space for honest self-awareness without defense or self-deception.

## Mindfulness and Meditation

Mindfulness practices and meditation can be powerful tools to deepen self-awareness. Through regular practice, you learn to observe your thoughts and feelings without judgment and to create an inner space where self-knowledge becomes possible.

You don't have to sit on a cushion for hours. Even a few minutes of daily mindfulness practice can make a noticeable difference.

## Body Awareness and Movement

Last but not least, good body awareness is also an important aspect of self-awareness. Through conscious movement such as yoga, tai chi, dancing, or even simply walking in nature, you can strengthen the connection to your body and learn to better understand its signals.

The body doesn't lie—it often shows us very clearly what we need or what burdens us, long before we become aware of it. Good body awareness is therefore a valuable key to deeper self-awareness overall.

## Practical Exercises: Your Path to Self-Awareness

Theory is important—but only practical implementation brings real change. Here you'll find concrete exercises that will help you deepen your self-awareness. Choose the ones that appeal to you and integrate them into your daily life.

### Exercise 1: The Daily Check-In

Take five minutes three times a day (morning, noon, evening) for a short check-in with yourself. Ask yourself the following questions and answer them honestly:

- How do I feel physically right now? (Energized, tired, tense, relaxed...)

- How do I feel emotionally? (Happy, sad, angry, anxious, content...)

- What's occupying my thoughts? (Worries, plans, memories...)

- What do I need right now? (Rest, movement, conversation, nourishment...)

Note your answers briefly in a small notebook. Over time, you'll recognize patterns and get to know yourself better.

### Exercise 2: The Values Interview

Conduct an interview with yourself about your values. Ask yourself the following questions and take time for honest, in-depth answers:

- What is truly important to me in life?

- What would I stand up for, even if it's uncomfortable?

- What constitutes a successful life for me?

- When I look back on my life from a distant future, what do I want to be proud of?

- Which three values are most important to me? (e.g., freedom, connection, creativity, security, adventure...)

This exercise helps you gain clarity about your values—an important part of your personality core.

## Exercise 3: The Strengths Discovery Journey

Many people have a distorted view of themselves and primarily perceive their weaknesses. This exercise helps you discover your strengths:

1. Ask three people who know you well what they appreciate about you and what strengths they see in you.

2. Think about situations in your life that you've mastered well. What helped you do so?

3. Consider which activities come easily to you and bring you joy.

4. Pay attention for a week to compliments that are given to you.

Note all the strengths you discover and read through the list regularly to get a more balanced view of yourself.

## Exercise 4: The Needs Detection Aid

Many people have lost touch with their own needs. This exercise helps you rediscover them:

1. Create a list of possible needs (e.g., rest, movement, contact, creativity, security, freedom...).

2. Check for each need whether and how well it is fulfilled in your current life.

3. Pay conscious attention for a week to how your mood changes depending on whether certain needs are met or not.

4. When you feel unwell, always ask yourself: "What do I need right now?"

Over time, you'll develop a finer sense for your needs and be able to perceive them earlier.

## Exercise 5: The Emotions Journal

Feelings are important signposts, but many people have forgotten how to perceive them. This exercise helps you sharpen your emotional self-awareness:

1. In the evening, note in a journal which emotions you experienced during the day.

2. Try to be as precise as possible (not just "good" or "bad," but e.g., "excitedly happy," "peaceful," "concerned," "irritated"...).

3. Pay attention to where in the body you felt the respective emotion.

4. Consider what triggered the emotion and what needs might be behind it.

Over time, you'll develop an increasingly fine sense for your emotional reactions and learn to understand them better.

## Exercise 6: The Body Awareness Meditation

This simple meditation helps you to perceive your body more consciously:

1. Sit comfortably or lie on your back.

2. Close your eyes and breathe deeply in and out a few times.

3. Direct your attention to your body and "scan" it from your feet to your head.

4. Notice where you feel tension, lightness, warmth, cold, pain, or other sensations.

5. Observe these sensations without judgment and without the impulse to change anything.

Do this exercise regularly, e.g., every morning or evening for 5-10 minutes.

## Exercise 7: The Life Roles Analysis

This exercise helps you recognize which roles you feel comfortable in and which you don't:

1. Make a list of all the roles you take on in your life (e.g., partner, parent, child, friend, colleague, supervisor, neighbor...).

2. Rate for each role on a scale of 1-10 how comfortable you feel in it.

3. For roles with low values, consider: What exactly doesn't feel right? What would need to change?

4. Check whether the roles that are important to you get enough space in your life.

This analysis helps you better understand in which areas of your life you lose yourself and where you can be completely authentic.

## Exercise 8: The Gratitude Practice

Gratitude is a special form of self-awareness that directs your gaze to the positive in your life:

1. Take five minutes every evening before going to bed.

2. Note three things from the day for which you are grateful—big or small.

3. Describe briefly why you are grateful for them and what feeling this gratitude evokes in you.

4. Read through your notes again and feel the gratitude.

Make this exercise a regular ritual. Neuroscientific and psychological research describes gratitude as an "impactful life attitude." Scientific studies, such as those by Michael McCullough and Robert Emmons, show that gratitude has a positive effect on the brain, health, and life satisfaction. It reduces stress, improves relationships, strengthens the heart, and demonstrably makes people happier.

All these exercises are tools to strengthen the foundation of your House of Self-Competence. They help you perceive yourself more clearly and thus create the basis for a stable, authentic life.

Remember: Self-awareness is not a one-time task, but a lifelong process. As with a real house, the foundation of self-competence must be regularly checked and maintained. With the exercises in this chapter, you have the necessary tools at hand.

In the next chapter, we will deal with the first supporting wall: self-acceptance. Because when self-awareness shows you what is, then the next step is to accept this current state—as a starting point for any change.

CHAPTER 2

# The First Supporting Wall - Self-Acceptance

---

*"The hardest task in life is to accept yourself as you are."*

---

## Self-Check: How's Your Self-Acceptance?

Before we dive into this important chapter, take a moment for an honest self-assessment. The following five characteristics indicate healthy self-acceptance. How many apply to you?

- You accept yourself as you are now—with all your strengths and all your weaknesses

- You forgive yourself for actual or perceived mistakes from your past

- You know that you cannot change anything in your past (whether positive or negative)

- You see your present self (without deficits) as a starting point for further growth
- You accept circumstances that you cannot change

The more of these statements you can answer with a clear "Yes," the more stable your first supporting wall already is. But don't worry if you hesitate on some or all points—that's what this chapter is for.

# Understanding Self-Acceptance and Self-Forgiveness

Imagine coming home and being greeted by a friend who looks at you and says: "Oh, there you are. Well, better than nothing. I mean, you're not perfect, but it could be worse. We definitely need to work on your flaws though."

How would you feel? Probably not particularly welcome or loved.

Yet this is exactly how many people speak to themselves—day after day, year after year. They stand in front of the mirror and see only their flaws. They look at their lives and focus on everything that didn't work out. They look at their personality and primarily notice aspects they interpret as weaknesses.

## The Core of Self-Acceptance

Greatly simplified, self-acceptance can be reduced to a simple sentence:

**"I am good—just as I am now."**

Just as I am now—that means with all my strengths and all my (perceived) weaknesses. With my history, my experiences, my characteristics, my body. With everything that makes me who I am, here and today.

This unconditional acceptance of your own self is something completely different from resignation or stagnation. It doesn't mean that no development is necessary or possible. On the contrary: It creates the prerequisite for healthy growth. The crucial difference is that you don't begin your further development from a feeling of deficit or lack.

This is important because it fundamentally changes the direction of motivation: It's no longer away from something ("I'm not good enough and need to get better"), but toward a positive goal ("I am good, and from this basis I can grow and develop").

## Accepting Circumstances

Self-acceptance also includes accepting unchangeable circumstances. Some things in our lives we can influence, others we cannot. There's a well-known saying: "Love it, leave it, or change it"—love it, leave it, or change it. We could add a fourth element: "Accept it"—accept it, at least for a certain time.

Not everything can be changed immediately, and some things cannot be changed at all. The art of self-acceptance also lies in making this distinction and making peace with the unchangeable aspects of life.

## Peace With the Past

A particularly important aspect of self-acceptance is making peace with your own past. Susanne's wise advice is: "You should give up hope for a better past."

How often do we torment ourselves with thoughts like "If only I had…," "If I only…," or "Why didn't I…?" These mental time travels are not only fruitless—they also rob us of energy for the here and now.

The truth is: Decisions made cannot be undone. Paths traveled cannot be untraveled. Things done cannot be undone. And that applies to both positive and negative experiences. Everything we've experienced has made us the person we are today.

What we can do is: Accept ourselves at the current state and, building on that, shape our present and future. This includes forgiving ourselves—for mistakes, for missed opportunities, for everything we reproach ourselves or others for.

### Self-Acceptance Is Not Self-Complacency

Sometimes self-acceptance is misunderstood as a kind of self-complacency or as an excuse not to develop further. "This is just how I am, you have to live with it" is not self-acceptance, but a refusal to work on oneself.

True self-acceptance includes the willingness to develop—but not from a place of lack, rather from a position of strength and self-worth. It says: "I am good as I am. And from this solid foundation, I can continue to develop."

## The Connection to the Foundation and Other Elements

As with a real house, in the House of Self-Competence, no element stands alone. Each is connected to the others and influences them—but is also influenced by them.

## No Acceptance Without Awareness

Self-acceptance can only succeed if we have an honest, authentic self-awareness. You must first perceive yourself as a person/personality to be able to accept yourself.

If your self-awareness is distorted—if you see yourself only through the filter of your weaknesses or have an unrealistic ideal image of yourself—then your self-acceptance will also stand on shaky ground. That's why it's so important that the foundation of self-awareness is strong and stable.

## Acceptance as a Basis for Empowerment

If your self-acceptance is only half-hearted, it will also be difficult for you to take self-empowerment—the second supporting wall of the house. If there are doubts about your self in you, these will transfer to your self-empowerment, and ultimately it will fail because of them.

Only when you fully accept yourself—with all your strengths and weaknesses, with your history and your potentials—can you also take full responsibility for your life.

## The Path to Self-Esteem

A healthy self-esteem with its three aspects (self-love, self-confidence, and self-assurance) cannot emerge without self-acceptance. How could you love yourself if you haven't accepted yourself first? How could you have confidence in yourself if you don't accept yourself in your entirety?

Self-acceptance is an essential prerequisite for self-esteem—it prepares the ground on which the roof of the house can rest.

### The Significance for Self-Care

Last but not least, self-acceptance also has a great influence on your ability for self-care. If you don't fully accept yourself, you won't be able to take good care of yourself either. You'll ignore or set aside your needs because you don't consider them legitimate or don't feel worthy of them.

Only when you fully accept yourself will it also become clear that you deserve to be well cared for—and you gain the necessary self-understanding to perceive and fulfill your needs.

## What Keeps Us from Self-Acceptance

The path to full self-acceptance is often not easy. There are numerous obstacles that can stand in our way—many of which we haven't chosen ourselves, but have adopted through upbringing, society, and life experiences.

### The Burden of Upbringing

Here again, upbringing plays an essential role. Those who heard a lot of criticism as a child will have deeply internalized these evaluations, often as belief and/or behavior patterns.

"You're too loud." "Don't be so sensitive." "You can't do that." "You'll never amount to anything."—Such statements leave deep traces in the child's psyche and make it difficult later to accept oneself.

Children who are constantly criticized for their behavior or even for their being develop a critical inner parent image that accompanies them into adulthood and constantly whispers to them that they are not good enough as they are.

34

## The Education System and Missed Strengths

Our education system can also lead to reduced self-acceptance, as all students must learn the same material—regardless of their individual inclinations, talents, and predispositions.

An illustrative example: No one knows paintings by Mozart, compositions by Einstein, or physical research by Picasso. All three consistently focused on their strengths. But that's exactly what school doesn't do!

Let's say Mozart were to come into our current school system. He would certainly be praised for his musical talent. But perhaps mathematical weaknesses would be discovered in him. The pedagogical energy would focus on bringing him to at least average performance in math. This would cost little Wolfgang-Amadeus strength and time—which in turn would prevent him from pursuing his true talent (music).

Unfortunately, our school system works exactly like this. Instead of promoting strengths, it tries to raise weaknesses to an average level. This significantly weakens self-acceptance because it sends us the message: "Your weaknesses are more important than your strengths."

## The Trap of Comparison

Comparing also proves to be extremely harmful here. Those who always compare themselves to others will inevitably feel worse (or inferior) and won't be able to accept themselves as they are.

The problem with comparisons is that we almost always compare upward—with people who are better than us in the respective area. Moreover, we often compare our weaknesses with the strengths of others, which inevitably leads to a negative result.

Social media acts like a turbo here as well. We see perfectly staged excerpts from the lives of others and compare them with our unedited, unfiltered everyday life. A comparison that can only turn out to the disadvantage of self-acceptance.

## Toxic Relationships

Private or business relationships can also negatively influence self-acceptance, especially relationships with narcissistic individuals, whose manipulative behavior can initially significantly affect the self-awareness and then the self-acceptance of their partners.

In such relationships, the self-image is systematically undermined. The partner conveys through direct criticism, subtle devaluations, or emotional manipulation the message: "You are not good enough as you are." Over time, this poison can penetrate deeply into self-awareness and self-acceptance.

## Perfectionism as a Self-Acceptance Killer

Perfectionism is also a reliable killer of self-acceptance. It often leads to chronic dissatisfaction and thus weakening of self-acceptance.

For the perfectionist, nothing is ever good enough—especially not themselves. There's always something to improve, optimize, correct. This constant focus on what's not yet perfect prevents the acceptance of the current state and leads to a permanent feeling of inadequacy.

Perfectionists live in a world where self-acceptance is impossible because their own standards are so high that they can never be reached.

## The Societal Ideals

Our society constantly bombards us with ideal images—from the perfect body to the perfect career to the perfect relationship. These ideals are so omnipresent that we often unconsciously adopt them and begin to measure ourselves against them.

The problem: These ideals are usually unrealistic and often even contradictory. We're supposed to be successful and relaxed at the same time, socially engaged and career-focused, self-confident and modest. These unfulfillable expectations make it difficult to accept yourself as you are.

## What Promotes Self-Acceptance

As numerous as the obstacles may be—there are just as many factors that can promote healthy self-acceptance. With the right conditions and practices, everyone can learn to accept themselves more fully.

### The Power of Early Reinforcement

When children were authentically praised and supported in their strengths, they usually also have a significantly better developed self-acceptance as adults.

Children who receive the message: "You are good as you are. Your strengths are valuable. Your weaknesses are a part of you, but they don't define you"—these children have much better prerequisites later to accept themselves.

But even if you didn't receive these messages as a child, it's not too late. You can begin now to give yourself these messages and thus strengthen your self-acceptance.

## A Supportive Environment

An appreciative family and professional environment also makes it easier to develop and maintain good self-acceptance.

People who accept you as you are, who see and appreciate your strengths, who don't constantly criticize or want to change you—they are like fertile soil on which your self-acceptance can grow.

Surround yourself, as far as possible, with people who support you in your self-acceptance, and reduce contact with people who constantly criticize or devalue you.

## The Focus on Strengths

A conscious focus on your own strengths can significantly promote self-acceptance. Instead of constantly dealing with your weaknesses, take time to recognize, appreciate, and use your strengths.

This focus doesn't mean that you ignore your weaknesses—it's more about developing a balanced image of yourself, in which strengths and weaknesses equally have a place and are accepted.

## The Power of Gratitude

Gratitude can be a powerful tool for more self-acceptance. When you regularly reflect on the things in your life for which you are grateful—including your own characteristics and abilities—you create an attitude of appreciation that also includes yourself.

Gratitude directs attention to what is (instead of what is missing), and thus creates a basis for genuine self-acceptance.

## The Practice of Mindfulness

Mindfulness practices can help you perceive yourself without judgment and thus find deeper self-acceptance. Through regular mindfulness exercises, you learn to observe your thoughts, feelings, and body sensations without immediately evaluating or changing them.

This non-judgmental observation is the first step to acceptance— only when you perceive without judging can you truly accept what is.

## The Insight into Shared Humanity

An important realization that promotes self-acceptance is the awareness of our shared humanity. Yes, you have weaknesses, make mistakes, have fears and insecurities—but so do all humans.

This insight takes the sting out of not being perfect. It's not a personal failure, but part of the human experience. In this awareness, it becomes easier to accept yourself with all your facets.

# The Social Aspect of Self-Acceptance

Self-acceptance not only has effects on our personal well-being, but also on our coexistence with other people. It fundamentally changes how we approach others and interact with them.

## From Self-Acceptance to Acceptance of Others

If the sentence "I am good—just as I am now" applies to yourself, then logically it also applies to your fellow humans. They too are good—just as they are now.

This realization has the potential to transform our relationships. When we approach other people with this basic attitude, a lot changes. We no longer meet others with criticism, prejudices, or the desire to change them, but with acceptance and appreciation.

## The Vision of an Accepting Community

Imagine a family or a company where many (perhaps even all) interact with this attitude of acceptance. The gain in mutual appreciation would significantly improve the quality of life for all involved.

There would be no more gossiping or talking behind the backs of other people, because other people would be okay in their way. There would be fewer conflicts, fewer misunderstandings, fewer disappointments—because everyone accepts the other as they are, instead of expecting them to change.

Admittedly, this is a vision. But it's a beautiful vision—and it begins with your own self-acceptance.

## The Path to More Tolerance and Compassion

Self-acceptance is also the breeding ground for more tolerance and compassion in our society. When we learn to accept ourselves with all our edges and corners, we also become more tolerant and compassionate towards others.

This expanded perspective allows us to see differences not as a threat, but as an enrichment. It helps us to break out of the tight corset of "right" and "wrong" and to appreciate the diversity of human being.

## Exercises for More Self-Acceptance in Everyday Life

Theory is important—but only practical implementation brings real change. Here you'll find concrete exercises that will help you deepen your self-acceptance. Choose the ones that appeal to you and integrate them into your daily life.

### Exercise 1: Daily Autosuggestion

The French pharmacist Émile Coué discovered over 100 years ago the amazing power of autosuggestion—the targeted positive self-influence through repetition of affirming sentences.

Here's how:

1. Choose a sentence like "I am valuable because I am me" or "I accept myself completely, with all strengths and weaknesses."

2. Speak this sentence out loud three times in the morning and three times in the evening.

3. Make sure to speak it gently, lovingly, and mindfully—as if you were speaking to a beloved person.

4. Do this exercise for at least 60 to 90 days to create a new neural connection in your brain.

This simple practice can change your unconscious beliefs about yourself over time and thus lead to deeper self-acceptance.

## Exercise 2: The Mirror Exercise

This exercise may seem unusual at first, but it is a powerful tool to strengthen your self-acceptance.

Here's how:

1. Stand naked in front of a large mirror (make sure you are undisturbed). It's not about examining your body, but about removing the protective shell of clothing.

2. Look your mirror image in the eyes concentratedly for 5 minutes.

3. After 5 minutes, continue to look into the eyes and say to the person in the mirror: "I love you. Exactly as you are now."

Caution: This exercise can be emotionally intense. It should not be performed in cases of severe depression, suicidal thoughts, or psychotic disorders. If you have strong emotional reactions, stop the exercise and contact a therapist or another trusted person.

## Exercise 3: The Gratitude Ritual

Self-acceptance and gratitude go hand in hand. This exercise combines well with the journal exercise from the chapter on self-awareness.

Here's how:

1. Take a moment every evening before going to bed.

2. Speak aloud or in your thoughts the following sentences: "Thank you for letting me be me. Just as I am now. Just as it is now. In this moment. Thank you."

3. Feel how these words feel in your body.

This exercise sounds a bit like a prayer, but you don't have to be religious to benefit from it. It creates an attitude of gratitude and acceptance towards yourself and your life as it is now.

## Exercise 4: The Letter to Your Younger Self

This exercise helps you make peace with your past and approach yourself with more compassion.

Here's how:

1. Choose an age from your past when you had a particularly difficult time.

2. Write a letter to your younger self at this age.

3. Express in the letter all the understanding, compassion, and acceptance that you perhaps didn't experience back then.

4. Don't hold back—write everything that your younger self would have needed in your opinion.

5. Read the letter aloud as if you were speaking to this younger self.

This exercise can be very healing and help you close old wounds and develop greater acceptance for your entire life story.

## Exercise 5: The Strengths Collage

This creative exercise helps you focus on your strengths and thus strengthen your self-acceptance.

Here's how:

1. Collect images, words, quotes, symbols—anything that represents your strengths, talents, and positive characteristics.
2. Create a collage from these materials on a large sheet of paper.
3. Hang the finished collage in a place where you see it daily.
4. Each time you see it, take a moment to feel and appreciate the strengths depicted.

This visual reminder of your strengths can help you develop a more balanced self-image and accept yourself more easily in your entirety.

## Exercise 6: The Acceptance Meditation

This meditation helps you cultivate an attitude of acceptance towards yourself and your life.

Here's how:

1. Sit comfortably and close your eyes.
2. Breathe deeply in and out a few times to calm down.

3. Then speak internally or softly the following sentences, pausing after each sentence to really feel it:

- "I accept my body as it is now."
- "I accept my thoughts as they are now."
- "I accept my feelings as they are now."
- "I accept my past as it was."
- "I accept my life as it is now."
- "I accept myself as I am now."

4. After the meditation, take another moment to feel how this acceptance feels in your body.

This meditation can be practiced regularly to cultivate a deeper attitude of self-acceptance.

## Exercise 7: The Self-Forgiveness Practice

This exercise helps you forgive yourself and thus find deeper self-acceptance.

Here's how:

1. Think of something you haven't yet forgiven yourself for—a decision, an action, an omission.

2. Write down exactly what you reproach yourself for and why.

3. Now imagine a loved one had done exactly the same thing and would ask you for forgiveness. What would you say to him or her?

4. Write down these words of forgiveness and then direct them at yourself.

5. Conclude with a concrete act of self-forgiveness, e.g., by ritually burning what you've written or by saying aloud: "I forgive myself."

This exercise can be particularly effective in dissolving old feelings of guilt and finding a deeper acceptance of your entire life story.

All these exercises are tools to strengthen the first supporting wall of your House of Self-Competence. They help you accept yourself more fully and thus create the basis for a stable, authentic life.

Remember: Self-acceptance is not a one-time task, but a continuous process. As with a real house, this wall must also be regularly checked and repaired if necessary. With the exercises in this chapter, you have the necessary tools at hand.

In the next chapter, we will deal with the second supporting wall: self-empowerment. Because if self-acceptance helps you accept your current state, then self-empowerment gives you the power to actively shape your life from this basis.

# CHAPTER 3

# The Second Supporting Wall - Self-Empowerment

---

*"The price of greatness is responsibility."*

– Winston Churchill

---

## Self-Check: How's Your Self-Empowerment?

Before we dive into this important chapter, take a moment for an honest self-assessment. The following characteristics indicate a strong self-empowerment. How many apply to you?

- You take responsibility for your life and are aware that you can actively make a difference through your actions

- You don't blame others when things don't go as you wish in your life

- Your life is your area of decision (or in sporting terms: your playing field)

- You know that your decisions have consequences, and you are ready to bear them
- You recognize that you are not responsible for everything, but for your response to everything

The more of these statements you can answer with a clear "Yes," the more stable your second supporting wall already is. But don't worry if you hesitate on some or all points—that's what this chapter is for.

## Self-Empowerment and Self-Efficacy Defined

When people fail to strengthen their self-competence, it's usually precisely here: at self-empowerment. "I had no choice." "The others are to blame." "Nothing can be done. That's just how I am."

You may have heard these sentences from others—or even thought or spoken them yourself. They sound harmless, but they are actually small declarations of surrender. With each of these sentences, we give up a piece of our power to shape our lives.

### What Does Self-Empowerment Mean?

Self-empowerment means that you take on the authorship of your life. You recognize that your life is primarily the result of your decisions and actions—not the result of external circumstances or the behavior of other people.

It doesn't mean that you're responsible for everything that happens to you. No one has complete control over all circumstances of life. But it does mean that you take responsibility for your response to these circumstances.

Self-empowerment also means bearing the consequences of your decisions. Every decision FOR something is simultaneously a decision AGAINST something else. If I decide on a certain job, I'm deciding against all other possible jobs. If I decide on a relationship, I'm deciding against being single (or for another relationship). Accepting these consequences is an essential part of self-empowerment.

## The Connection to Self-Efficacy

Closely linked to self-empowerment is self-efficacy—the conviction that you can make a difference through your own actions. While self-empowerment is the willingness to stand up for your own life, self-efficacy is the belief in your own ability to change things and achieve goals.

These two elements reinforce each other: The more you believe in your ability to act effectively, the easier it is for you to take responsibility. And the more responsibility you take, the more experiences of self-efficacy you have.

## Taking Responsibility vs. Giving Away Responsibility

It's surprisingly easy for us to give away responsibility, even though in doing so, we're handing over an essential control element for our lives. Why do we do this?

One reason is that taking responsibility also means bearing consequences. Perhaps we have to admit mistakes, apologize, accept disadvantages. Perhaps we even have to disappoint people who are important to us. Many shy away from precisely this.

Another reason is that it can be comfortable in the short term to give away responsibility. If "the circumstances" or "the others" are to blame, we don't have to change anything, risk anything, make an effort. In the long run, however, we pay a high price for this: We lose control over our lives and fall into a victim role that weakens us and makes us unhappy.

## Why Self-Empowerment Is a Source of Strength

Self-empowerment may initially seem like a burden—all these decisions, all these consequences! In reality, however, it is one of the greatest sources of strength we have. Why is that?

### From Victim to Creator

When you take responsibility for your life, you undertake a fundamental role change: from passive victim to active creator. This is an enormous shift in perspective and energy.

As a victim, you feel at the mercy of circumstances. You react instead of acting. You lament what is, instead of creating what could be. This attitude robs you of energy and joy in life.

As a creator, on the other hand, you take the helm of your life. You recognize your room for maneuver and use it. You focus on solutions instead of problems. This attitude gives you energy and a feeling of self-efficacy.

### The Freedom of Choice

Self-empowerment is closely linked to the realization that you always have a choice. Perhaps not regarding the circumstances, but in any case regarding your response to these circumstances.

Viktor Frankl, the founder of logotherapy, gained this insight during his time in a concentration camp: "Between stimulus and response, there is a space. In that space lies our power to choose our response. In our response lie our development and our freedom."

This freedom of choice is an enormous source of strength. It frees you from the victim role and gives you the opportunity to decide anew in each situation how you want to react to it.

## Strengthening Self-Esteem

Taking responsibility strengthens your self-esteem. When you recognize that you can shape your life, when you achieve successes and also accept failures as part of your path, a deep feeling of self-respect emerges.

This feeling is not dependent on external confirmation or perfect results. It arises from the knowledge that you face the challenges of life and do your best—regardless of whether everything works out as you imagined in the end.

## The Power to Change

Perhaps the greatest empowerment of self-empowerment is the realization that change is possible. When you take responsibility for your life, you recognize that you are not stuck in your current situation, your habits, or your relationship patterns.

You can make new decisions, go new ways, practice new behaviors. This realization is incredibly liberating and energizing. It opens doors that previously seemed locked and shows possibilities that were previously invisible.

# Typical Blockades of Self-Empowerment

As powerful as self-empowerment is—there are numerous blockades that can prevent us from fully taking it on. Some of these blockades are deeply rooted in our psyche, others are reinforced by social influences.

## The Victim Role

One of the strongest blockades is the victim role—the conviction that we are at the mercy of circumstances or other people and have no control over our lives.

The victim role can be very seductive. It relieves us of responsibility and gives us, in the short term, the good feeling of being right ("The others are to blame!"). It can even bring us attention and sympathy.

In the long term, however, the victim role is a trap. It makes us passive, helpless, and dependent on external circumstances or other people. It prevents us from discovering our own strength and ability to act.

## External Control Beliefs

Closely related to the victim role are external control beliefs—the belief that our life is mainly controlled by external factors: luck or bad luck, fate, powerful other people, social structures.

People with strong external control beliefs often feel powerless. They don't believe that they can make a difference through their own actions, and therefore don't take responsibility for their lives either. Instead, they wait for circumstances to change or for someone else to solve their problems.

## Fear of Consequences

Another common blockade is the fear of the consequences of our decisions. Taking responsibility means acknowledging that our decisions have consequences—and that not all of these consequences are pleasant.

This fear can be so strong that we prefer not to make a decision at all (which is of course also a decision!) or that we shift the responsibility for our decisions onto others. This way, we try to escape the fear—but actually, we only strengthen it by experiencing ourselves as incapable of acting.

## Self-Sabotage and Habit Patterns

Self-sabotaging behaviors and ingrained habit patterns can also be strong blockades to self-empowerment. These patterns are often deeply rooted and partly unconscious.

Perhaps you repeatedly have relationships with similar (unsuitable) partners. Or you sabotage professional opportunities by missing deadlines or provoking conflicts. Or you repeatedly resort to unhealthy coping strategies in stressful situations, such as eating, alcohol, or excessive media consumption.

Recognizing and changing these patterns requires a high degree of self-empowerment—and at the same time, they can block the taking on of this responsibility because they keep us in a reactive rather than a proactive stance.

## Perfectionism and Fear of Mistakes

Perfectionism can be a subtle but effective blockade to self-empowerment. If we believe that we must be perfect and must not make mistakes, we will either not act at all (out of fear of failing) or we will deny responsibility for our decisions in case of failures (because we cannot bear the failure).

Real self-empowerment means acknowledging that mistakes and failures are part of the path. They are not the end, but learning opportunities that take us further.

## Social and Cultural Influences

Finally, social and cultural influences can also make it difficult to take on self-empowerment. In a society that strongly focuses on external factors for success and happiness (money, status, possessions, external appearance), it can be hard to look inward and recognize your own responsibility.

Cultural imprints such as strong collectivism (the group is more important than the individual) or a belief in fate can also hinder the development of self-empowerment.

## Formative Parenting Styles

Self-empowerment is also strongly influenced in its development by upbringing—interestingly, by two very different but equally problematic parenting styles.

On the one hand, there is the authoritarian upbringing: The child is told what to do, what is right and what is wrong. In this environment, the child does not have sufficient opportunity to make their own decisions and experience their consequences. They learn to obey authorities, instead of taking responsibility themselves. As an adult, it is then difficult to make independent decisions and to bear the responsibility for them.

On the other hand, there is the parenting style of so-called "helicopter parents." To provide their offspring with the most worry-free youth possible, these parents clear all obstacles out of the way, try to prevent conflicts from arising in the first place, or solve them themselves, instead of giving the child the opportunity to learn responsibility.

This is well-meant, but ultimately produces children who, as adults, find it very difficult to take responsibility for themselves and their lives. How could they know how? Mom and Dad always took care of that. Without the experience that one's own decisions have consequences—both positive and negative—no real self-empowerment can develop.

## The Technology Trap

Technological progress is great in many ways. However, it has a price: The more modern technology automates and controls our lives, the more we humans lose the feeling for our self-empowerment.

We trust a fitness tracker that tells us what is healthy for us, instead of listening to our body. We let ourselves be supported by various assistance systems in the car, instead of being attentive ourselves. Smart devices and artificial intelligence make more and more decisions for us—from music taste to the route in traffic.

All of this is very practical, but we lose a bit of our own perception on the one hand, and on the other hand, we are released from self-empowerment. The consequence is a creeping erosion of our ability and willingness to take real responsibility.

## The Spiritual Excuse

Spirituality is something wonderful and should by no means be portrayed negatively here. However, it becomes problematic when cosmic phenomena are used as an explanation for why there is a lack of self-empowerment.

"It's portal days right now. Nothing can be done." Or: "I'm a Scorpio, I can't help it." Such statements may be comforting because they relieve us of responsibility for our behavior—but that's exactly the problem.

Similarly, when the "inner child" (a concept originally developed in a psychological context) is used as an excuse for certain behaviors. Of course, early experiences shape us strongly, but that doesn't absolve us of responsibility for our actions today.

Religion can also play a role here. Faith can be something very empowering. However, if "God's will" is cited as an excuse for a lack of self-empowerment, it is problematic. Then a potentially strengthening spiritual practice becomes a blockade to self-empowerment.

All these external control beliefs have one thing in common: They shift control and thus responsibility outward—and thus rob us of our power to shape our own lives.

# Factors That Strengthen Self-Empowerment

As numerous as the blockades may be—there are just as many factors that can strengthen our self-empowerment. With the right attitudes and practices, everyone can learn to take more responsibility for their lives.

## Awareness of Room for Maneuver

An important factor is the awareness of our room for maneuver. In many situations, we have more options than we are aware of. The question "What can I do in this situation?" opens our eyes to these possibilities and activates our ability to act.

Even in very restricted situations, there is almost always room for your own decisions—if only the decision on how you want to deal with the situation internally.

## Focus on Solutions Instead of Problems

A solution-oriented focus greatly strengthens self-empowerment. Instead of asking yourself "Why is this happening to me?" or "Who is to blame?", better ask yourself "What can I do now?" or "What solution is possible?"

This shift in focus brings about a fundamental change: from a reactive, problem-fixated attitude to a proactive, solution-oriented attitude. It activates your creativity and your ability to act.

## Successes and Self-Efficacy Experiences

Nothing strengthens self-empowerment as much as the experience that your actions actually make a difference—that you can shape your life through your decisions and actions.

Begin with small steps, set achievable goals, and celebrate your successes. Every positive experience of self-efficacy strengthens your confidence in your ability to take responsibility and shape your life.

## A Supportive Environment

An environment that supports you in your self-empowerment can make an enormous difference. People who believe in you, who encourage you to take responsibility, and who don't push you into a victim role—they can help you strengthen your second supporting wall.

Surround yourself, as far as possible, with people who themselves take responsibility for their lives and who inspire you to do the same. Avoid people who are constantly in victim mode and who also want to pull you into this role.

## Reflection and Self-Knowledge

Regular reflection can significantly strengthen your self-empowerment. Take time to think about your life, recognize patterns, learn from experiences.

Ask yourself: Where do I already take responsibility for my life? Where do I still give away responsibility? What blockades prevent me from taking full responsibility? What could help me overcome these blockades?

This kind of reflection sharpens your awareness of your own role in your life and helps you take more responsibility.

## The Power of Clear Decisions

Clear, conscious decisions directly strengthen your self-empowerment. Every time you make a decision—instead of hesitating, avoiding, or leaving the decision to others—you exercise your "responsibility muscle."

Begin with small decisions and work your way up to bigger ones. Make sure that your decisions are really your own—not imposed by others or made out of a sense of obligation.

## Practical Impulses: How to Take Responsibility for Your Life

Theory is important—but only practical implementation brings real change. Here you'll find concrete exercises that will help you strengthen your self-empowerment. Choose the ones that appeal to you and integrate them into your daily life.

### Exercise 1: The Language of Responsibility

Our language often reflects our inner attitude—and can influence it at the same time. Thi!s exercise helps you develop a language of responsibility.

Here's how:

1. Pay conscious attention to your language for a week: How often do you use formulations that give away responsibility? For example: "I had to...," "I had no choice...," "XY made me...," "Because of XY, I couldn't..."

2. Note these formulations and consider what a responsible alternative might sound like for each. For example: "I decided...," "I chose...," "I want...," "I will..."

3. Consciously practice using these new formulations in your everyday life.

This changed language may feel unfamiliar at first, but over time it will influence your inner attitude and help you take more responsibility for your life.

## Exercise 2: The Circle of Responsibility

This exercise helps you distinguish more clearly what you are responsible for and what not.

Here's how:

1. Draw two concentric circles on a sheet of paper—a smaller one in the middle and a larger one around it.

2. The inner circle represents your area of influence—everything you can directly influence: your thoughts, feelings, decisions, actions.

3. The outer circle represents your area of concern—everything you worry about, but cannot directly influence: the weather, the economy, the decisions of other people, past events.

4. Enter concrete examples from your life in both circles.

5. Reflect: How much of your energy do you invest in the outer circle? How could you direct more energy to the inner circle?

This exercise sharpens your awareness of where real responsibility lies, and helps you invest your energy more meaningfully.

## Exercise 3: The Decision Matrix

This exercise helps you make more conscious decisions and thus take more responsibility for your life.

Here's how:

1. When facing a decision, draw a matrix with four fields.
2. Label the fields with: "If I do X, Y positive happens" / "If I do X, Z negative happens" / "If I don't do X, A positive happens" / "If I don't do X, B negative happens".
3. Fill in all four fields by envisioning possible consequences of your decision.
4. Weight the individual points according to their importance to you.
5. Make a conscious decision based on this analysis.

This exercise helps you see the consequences of your decisions more clearly and take responsibility for them.

## Exercise 4: The Responsibility Journal

This exercise helps you develop a deeper awareness of your responsibility in everyday life.

Here's how:

1. Keep a journal for a week in which you answer the following questions every evening:
   - What did I take responsibility for today?

- Where did I give away responsibility today?
- What consequences did this have for me and others?
- With the knowledge of today, what would I do differently tomorrow?

2. At the end of the week, read through your entries again and reflect: What patterns do you recognize? What would you like to change?

This exercise sharpens your awareness of your daily decisions and their consequences.

## Exercise 5: The "What Can I Do?" Practice

This simple exercise helps you switch from the victim role to a proactive stance in difficult situations.

Here's how:

1. Whenever you feel powerless, frustrated, or like a victim of circumstances, consciously ask yourself the question: "What can I do in this situation?"
2. Write down at least three possible courses of action, no matter how small they may seem.
3. Choose one of these options and implement it.

This exercise activates your awareness of your room for maneuver and strengthens your self-efficacy.

## Exercise 6: The Mentor Conversation

This exercise helps you change perspectives and gain more clarity about your responsibility.

Here's how:

1. Think of a situation in which you are unsure whether or how to take responsibility.

2. Imagine a good friend coming to you with exactly the same problem. What would you advise him or her?

3. Or imagine that you were your own wise mentor. What would this mentor advise you?

4. Note these pieces of advice and consider how you could implement them.

This exercise uses the fact that we often see more clearly when it comes to the problems of others, and transfers this clarity to our own situation.

## Exercise 7: The 100% Responsibility

This exercise challenges you to take 100% responsibility in a certain area of your life for a limited time.

Here's how:

1. Choose an area of your life in which you want to take more responsibility (e.g., health, finances, a certain relationship).

2. Commit to taking 100% responsibility in this area for a week. This means: No excuses, no blame, no "I had no choice" sentences.

3. Keep a journal of your experiences: What changes when you take full responsibility? What obstacles appear? How does it feel?

4. After the week, reflect: What have you learned? What would you like to maintain?

This exercise can be a transformative experience that shows you how much power lies in the full taking of responsibility.

All these exercises are tools to strengthen the second supporting wall of your House of Self-Competence. They help you take more responsibility for your life and thus create the basis for a self-determined, fulfilled life.

Remember: Self-empowerment is not a one-time task, but a continuous process. As with a real house, this wall must also be regularly checked and repaired if necessary. With the exercises in this chapter, you have the necessary tools at hand.

In the next chapter, we will deal with the stabilizing support: self-care. Because only when you take good care of yourself can the supporting walls of self-acceptance and self-empowerment remain permanently stable.

# CHAPTER 4

# The Central Support - Self-Care

---

*"Only those who nourish their own source can fill others with life."*

---

## Self-Check: How's Your Self-Care?

Before we dive into this important chapter, take a moment for an honest self-assessment. The following characteristics indicate healthy self-care. How many apply to you?

- You regularly take time—just for yourself
- You know what's good for you
- You know your boundaries and how to defend them
- Stress doesn't stress you out—you can handle it
- You fall asleep easily and sleep peacefully through the night

The more of these statements you can answer with a clear "Yes," the more stable your central support already is. But don't worry if you hesitate on some or all points—that's what this chapter is for.

## What Does Real Self-Care Mean?

If you search the internet for the term "self-care," you mostly find endless lists telling you what you "must" do for good self-care. Yoga, meditation, journaling, forest bathing, digital detox... the list of recommendations is so long that you might immediately give up discouraged. As if self-care were just another to-do list in our already overfull lives.

But true self-care is the opposite of working through lists. Self-care is above all one thing: individual!

### Beyond the Lists – Your Personal Path

What's super helpful for one person can be pure stress for another. A personal example: A few years ago, we met a woman in France whom we estimated to be in her mid-40s. She mentioned casually that she had just had a milestone birthday, and we started pondering. For 50, she looked clearly too young, for 40, a little bit too old. We were all the more surprised when she finally told us that she had just turned 60!

Of course, we wanted to know the secret of her youthful appearance. Her answer: "J'aime la vie"—I love life!

She told us that she takes very good care of herself and does what relaxes and fulfills her with joy. In her case, that was... gardening. What is a tedious duty for others was pure self-care for her.

This example shows what real self-care is about: not about what you "should" do, but about what personally does you good, what nourishes, fulfills, and strengthens you.

## Self-Care versus Self-Optimization

An important distinction that is often overlooked: Self-care is not the same as self-optimization. Selfies at yoga showing others how "cool" you take care of yourself have just as little to do with genuine self-care as obsessive performance tracking on the smart watch.

Self-care SHOULD do you good—without performance pressure and without seeking validation externally. It's not a performance for others, but a gift to yourself.

Of course, you can track your performance during sports and challenge yourself again and again. But that has nothing to do with self-care—then it's called "training." A movement therapist friend once said: "If you can't smile during your activity anymore, then it's not self-care."

This simple criterion—can you smile while doing it?—is a good measure to distinguish whether an activity truly serves your self-care or whether it stems from other motives, such as the pursuit of recognition or self-optimization.

## Body, Mind, and Soul

Classically, it's said that in self-care, you should equally take care of soul, body, and mind. But this too is an ideal that doesn't apply equally to all people.

A passionate athlete with a high urge to move might experience exactly the opposite of relaxation during a silent meditation. An intellectual person might find more recreation in a good book than in a yoga class. And a highly sensitive person might need more withdrawal and quiet than someone who draws energy from social contacts.

In this respect, self-care is closely linked to self-awareness—it's about finding out what could do you good right now. And then self-empowerment comes into play, because it's about actually doing it. This in turn strengthens self-esteem, because you are worth taking time for yourself.

This shows how all elements of the House of Self-Competence are connected and strengthen each other.

## Realistic Times for Self-Care

How much time should one take for healthy self-care? On the internet, an hour a day is often mentioned. But let's be honest: That's not realistically feasible for managers or single parents.

The good news is: Self-care doesn't have to be time-consuming to be effective. Sometimes just five conscious breaths, a short walk around the block, or a phone call with a good friend are enough to recharge your batteries a bit.

What's decisive is not the duration, but the regularity and quality of self-care—the question of whether it really suits you and does you good.

## Self-Care as a Support for Your House

In our model of the house, self-care is an important support. Without it, the house would initially still stand. Over time, however, it would become unstable and, in the worst case, suffer serious damage.

It's the same with us humans: We function quite well for a while—until we eventually can't anymore. Until the body strikes, the psyche rebels, or the mind loses its clarity. To prevent it from getting that far, it's necessary to regularly do something that's good for your body, your soul, or your mind.

## More than Wellness – The Two Pillars of Self-Care

Self-care includes not only the pleasant, nourishing activities that we often associate with the term. It also encompasses two other, often overlooked aspects:

1. **Setting Boundaries**: The ability to set boundaries and say "No" when something becomes too much or doesn't feel right.
2. **Stress Management**: The competence to deal with unavoidable burdens in such a way that they cause as little damage as possible.

These two facets of self-care are at least as important as the regenerating activities—and often even more important because they work preventively and prevent us from getting into a state of exhaustion in the first place.

Real self-care is thus a holistic concept that includes both active regeneration and protection against overload. It's not a luxury, but a necessity—a central support that keeps your House of Self-Competence stable.

## The Stabilizing Power of Self-Care

Why is self-care such an essential support for our House of Self-Competence? What stabilizing power emanates from it?

## Protection Against Overload

Imagine driving a car without ever refueling, checking the tires, or changing the oil. How long would that go well? Probably not very long—and yet many people treat themselves exactly this way.

Self-care is like the regular maintenance of your body, mind, and soul. It protects you from overload by helping you replenish your resources in time, before they are exhausted.

When you regularly take care of yourself, you also notice earlier when something gets out of balance. You perceive warning signals such as tension, sleep disorders, or irritability earlier and can counteract before serious problems arise.

## Strengthening Resilience

Self-care strengthens your resilience—your psychological resistance. It helps you deal better with stress, crises, and challenges and recover from them more quickly.

A well-filled "inner battery" allows you to remain capable of acting even in difficult phases and not be overwhelmed by emotions or stress. You keep a clearer head and can react more appropriately.

This resilience acts like a buffer that cushions the effects of burdens and prevents them from directly impacting the supporting walls and the foundation of your house.

## Improving the Quality of Relationships

Good self-care also improves the quality of your relationships. When you take good care of yourself, you are less irritable, have more emotional capacity for others, and are less needy.

You can be more present and attentive, listen better, and empathize better with others. You are less dependent on others fulfilling your needs, and can thus lead more equal, healthier relationships.

Moreover, through good self-care, you set an example for others—especially important if you have children who learn from you how to treat themselves.

## Promoting Self-Acceptance

Self-care and self-acceptance—the first supporting wall—reinforce each other. When you take good care of yourself, you send yourself the message: "I am worth being cared for." This message strengthens your self-acceptance.

Conversely, good self-acceptance makes it easier to care for yourself. When you accept yourself with all your facets, you also recognize your needs and give yourself permission to fulfill them.

This positive interaction stabilizes the entire House of Self-Competence.

## Supporting Self-Empowerment

Self-care and self-empowerment—the second supporting wall—are also closely connected. Taking care of yourself is an act of taking responsibility for your well-being and your health.

You recognize that no one else is responsible for your well-being but yourself. And you act accordingly by making conscious decisions for your health and balance.

This exercise in self-empowerment strengthens your ability to take responsibility in other areas of life as well.

## The Basis for Self-Esteem

Finally, self-care also creates a solid basis for healthy self-esteem— the roof of our house. If you are important enough to yourself to take good care of yourself, a deep feeling of self-worth builds up over time.

You experience yourself as someone who deserves to be treated well—by yourself and by others. This experience strengthens your self-esteem in a very fundamental way.

Thus, it becomes clear why self-care is such a central support of our House of Self-Competence: It stabilizes all other elements and ensures that the house as a whole remains strong and resilient.

# What Prevents Healthy Self-Care?

As important as good self-care is—many people find it very difficult. What obstacles stand in the way of healthy self-care?

## The Myth of Selflessness

In many cultures and upbringing styles, selflessness is praised as a high virtue. Especially women often hear that it is noble to sacrifice oneself for others, and selfish to think of oneself.

This myth of selflessness leads to self-care being seen as selfish or luxurious—as something that one must first "earn," after all other obligations have been fulfilled.

What is overlooked here: Only those who take good care of themselves can also take good care of others in the long run. As in an airplane, the same applies in life: First put on your own oxygen mask, then help others.

## The Glorification of Busyness

Our society glorifies busyness and productivity. Those who are constantly busy are considered important and successful. Those who take breaks are seen as lazy or not committed enough.

This cultural imprint makes it difficult to give yourself permission to consciously slow down, take breaks, and plan time for regeneration. It feels like we're swimming against a strong societal current.

But especially in an accelerated world, conscious deceleration becomes an essential form of self-care.

## The Chronic Lack of Time

"I would like to take better care of myself, but I simply don't have time for it." We hear this sentence constantly in our practice—and it reflects the reality of many people.

Between professional demands, family obligations, social activities, and everyday organizational effort, there often remains little time for conscious self-care.

But especially when time is scarce, self-care becomes particularly important. It's then not about planning hour-long wellness rituals, but integrating small, realistic moments of self-care into everyday life.

## The Inability to Set Boundaries

Another major obstacle is the difficulty of setting boundaries and saying "No." Many people fear disappointing others, triggering conflicts, or not being liked if they set boundaries.

This fear leads to them repeatedly crossing their own boundaries, taking on too many obligations, and giving priority to the demands of others over their own needs.

But without the ability to set boundaries, healthy self-care becomes practically impossible.

## The Missing Self-Awareness

To be able to take good care of yourself, you must first know what you need and what's good for you. But many people have lost touch with their own needs.

They are so used to functioning and fulfilling the expectations of others that they no longer feel what they themselves need, what nourishes them, and what exhausts them.

Therefore, the development of good self-awareness—the foundation of our house—is an essential prerequisite for successful self-care.

## The Bad Conscience

Even if all practical obstacles are cleared away, many people still have a major inner obstacle: the bad conscience when they spend time and energy on themselves.

This bad conscience is often deeply rooted and connected with early messages like "Don't be selfish" or "Don't think so much about yourself." It can be so strong that it gives every form of self-care a bitter aftertaste and undermines its beneficial effect.

Overcoming this bad conscience is for many people the most important step towards healthy self-care.

## What Promotes Sustainable Self-Care?

Despite all these obstacles, there are ways to healthy, sustainable self-care. What factors can help you with this?

### Realistic Expectations

The first step to sustainable self-care is to develop realistic expectations. It's not about completing a perfect self-care program or implementing all the tips from wellness magazines.

Rather, it's about finding small, doable steps that fit into your life and that you can really integrate into your everyday life. A short walk during your lunch break is better than a one-hour workout that you never do because it doesn't fit into your schedule.

Begin with small changes that can be realistically implemented, and build on that.

### Giving Permission

Another important factor is to give yourself the explicit permission to take care of yourself. Many people unconsciously wait for someone else to give them this permission—a partner, a doctor, a therapist.

But ultimately, only you can give yourself this permission. You can decide that your well-being is important and that you are worth being treated well—by yourself and by others.

This inner permission is perhaps the most important factor for sustainable self-care.

## Seeking Support

Self-care doesn't have to be lonely. Seek support—be it through a partner, friends, a self-help group, or a coach or therapist.

This support can take various forms: practical help that gives you time for self-care; emotional support that encourages you to take care of yourself; or shared activities that make self-care a shared experience.

It's particularly effective if you work with someone who holds you accountable and asks whether you're really implementing your self-care intentions.

## Creating Structures

Sustainable self-care needs structure. Plan fixed times for self-care in your calendar and treat these appointments just as binding as professional or family obligations.

Develop routines and rituals that make self-care a self-evident part of your everyday life—like brushing your teeth or breakfast. The more self-care becomes a habit, the less willpower you need to implement it.

These structures give your self-care a fixed place in your life and make it more resistant to everyday stress.

## Training Self-Awareness

Good self-awareness is the foundation for effective self-care. Only when you feel what you need can you take good care of yourself.

Train your self-awareness by regularly pausing and asking yourself: How am I doing right now? What do I need now? What would do me good right now?

These conscious check-ins help you to perceive your needs earlier and respond to them more specifically, before you get into a state of exhaustion.

## Practicing Setting Boundaries

The ability to set boundaries is a central competence for sustainable self-care. Consciously practice saying "No" when something doesn't feel right or exceeds your capacities.

Begin with small, safe situations and work your way up to more difficult ones. Learn polite but clear formulations for your boundaries, and practice them in front of the mirror or with a trusted person.

Over time, setting boundaries becomes easier, and you'll notice that most people respect your boundaries when you communicate them clearly and in a friendly manner.

# Developing Everyday Self-Care Rituals

Theory is important—but only practical implementation brings real change. Here you'll find concrete suggestions on how to develop everyday self-care rituals. Choose those that appeal to you and integrate them into your daily life.

## Micro-Self-Care for Everyday Life

Self-care doesn't have to be time-consuming. Here are some ideas for small self-care moments that you can easily integrate into your everyday life:

- **The Three-Breaths-Moment**: Take time several times a day for three conscious, deep breaths. Feel how your body relaxes a bit more with each breath.

- **The Gratitude-Pause**: Pause briefly and name three things for which you are grateful in this moment. This small exercise shifts the focus from stress to appreciation.

- **The Body-Check-In**: Quickly scan your body from your feet to your head and notice where you feel tension. Consciously relax these areas as best you can.

- **The Senses-Refreshment**: Consciously activate one of your senses—smell a flower, briefly listen to a favorite song, touch something pleasant, taste a bite especially consciously.

- **The Mini-Timeout**: Treat yourself to a two-minute timeout in which you simply look out the window, close your eyes, or take a short fantasy journey.

These micro-practices may be brief, but their effect adds up over the day and can make a noticeable difference in your well-being.

## Movement or Relaxation? Or Both?

What's individually best for you, only you know. However, if you want to do something to reduce stress, you won't get around movement. Movement is scientifically proven to be a very effective means against stress.

It doesn't have to be a marathon run—perhaps you'll find gentle movement exercises that you can well integrate into your everyday life and that do you good. A short walk during your lunch break, some stretching exercises in between, or a spontaneous dance to your favorite song can already make a difference.

As for relaxation techniques, there are a variety of offerings: from Progressive Muscle Relaxation according to Jacobson to Autogenic Training to countless meditation techniques. Listen to your self-awareness and discover what's good for you.

Perhaps it's the combination of movement and relaxation that works best for you—such as Tai Chi, QiGong, or Yoga. These holistic practices combine physical activity with meditative elements and can be particularly effective in bringing body and mind into balance.

## Healthy Sleep as a Cornerstone of Self-Care

Sleep is vital for the regeneration of our body. Restful sleep is one of the most important aspects of self-care, which is unfortunately often neglected.

If you suffer from problems falling asleep or staying asleep, the following sleep hygiene measures can help:

- **Regular Bedtimes**: Try to go to bed and get up at the same time every day—even on weekends.

- **Sleep-Promoting Environment**: Ensure a dark, quiet, and pleasantly cool bedroom. Invest in a good mattress and comfortable bedding.

- **Digital Sunset**: Avoid blue light (smartphones, tablets, computers) at least one hour before bedtime.

- **Calming Evening Routine**: Develop a relaxing ritual before bedtime—such as a warm bath, light stretching exercises, or reading.

- **Mindfulness with Food and Drinks**: Avoid heavy meals, caffeine, and alcohol in the hours before bedtime.

If ruminating keeps you from falling asleep, the "rumination chair technique" can help: When you notice that you're ruminating in bed, get up, sit on a specific "rumination chair," and allow yourself to ruminate there for a limited time (e.g., 15 minutes). Then go back to bed—with the firm intention of limiting rumination to the chair. This technique helps to re-associate the bed with sleep instead of worries.

For persistent sleep problems, Cognitive Behavioral Therapy for Insomnia (CBT-I) can also help, a scientifically well-documented method that tackles sleep problems at the root. It includes techniques such as sleep restriction, stimulus control, and cognitive restructuring, which can help you find your way back to a healthy sleep pattern.

## The Morning and Evening Ritual

Self-care rituals in the morning and evening are particularly effective, framing your day and helping you to begin and end consciously.

A simple **morning ritual** could look like this:

- Before reaching for your smartphone, take a moment to take three deep breaths
- Ask yourself a positive question for the day, e.g., "What am I looking forward to today?"
- Drink a glass of water to gently activate your body
- Stretch and extend your body for one to two minutes

A calming **evening ritual** could include:

- Put away digital devices an hour before bedtime
- A short reflection of the day: What went well? What am I grateful for?
- A small relaxation exercise, e.g., progressive muscle relaxation
- Drink a cup of calming tea or read a few pages in a book

These rituals create a gentle transition between sleep and activity and help you to begin and end the day more consciously.

## The Boundaries Exercise

An important self-care practice is practicing boundary setting. Here is a simple exercise that can help you with this:

1. Make a list of situations in which you often cross your boundaries or feel uncomfortable
2. Choose one of these situations and consider: What would be an appropriate boundary in this situation?

3. Formulate a clear, friendly sentence with which you could communicate this boundary

4. Practice this sentence in front of the mirror or with a trusted person

5. Apply it the next time the situation occurs

Begin with situations that are not too threatening, and gradually work your way up to more difficult ones. With each successful boundary setting, your self-confidence will grow.

## The Personal Energy Source List

Every person has individual activities that give them strength and increase their well-being. It's worth consciously identifying and using these.

Here's how to create your personal energy source list:

1. Take time to reflect and note all activities that do you good, relax you, or energize you

2. Categorize them by duration (5 minutes, 30 minutes, several hours)

3. Ensure that you have activities for different areas of life (body, mind, soul, relationships)

4. Choose at least one activity from each category that you can realistically integrate into your everyday life

5. Consciously plan these activities into your calendar

This list is your personal self-care menu, from which you can choose depending on need and available time.

## The Stress Management Toolkit

Stress is inevitable, but we can learn to deal with it better. A personal stress management toolkit can help:

1. **Quick Stress Reduction**: Techniques for acute stress situations, e.g., deep breathing (especially the humming breath), shaking, briefly stepping out of the situation

2. **Mental Strategies**: Perspective change, positive self-talk, relativizing ("Is this really so important?")

3. **Physical Relief**: Movement, relaxation techniques, sufficient sleep

4. **Emotional Regulation**: Naming feelings, writing a journal, talking with someone

5. **Preventive Measures**: Time management, setting priorities, organizing support

Put together your personal toolkit of techniques that work for you, and keep it handy for stressful times.

## The Weekly Self-Care Date

Besides daily micro-self-care, it's valuable to regularly reserve larger time windows for yourself—for example, in the form of a weekly "date with yourself."

Here's how to design your self-care date:

1. Reserve a fixed time period each week (e.g., Sunday morning or Wednesday evening)

2. Treat this appointment as just as important as a meeting with a valued friend

3.  Plan in advance what you want to do with this time—something that nourishes and fulfills you

4.  Ensure that you are undisturbed (phone off, family informed)

5.  Be fully present in this time and consciously enjoy it

This regular date with yourself sends a powerful message: You are worth receiving time and attention—from yourself and from others.

## The Self-Care Community

Self-care doesn't have to be a lonely affair. A self-care community can motivate and support you:

1.  Find a "self-care buddy" with whom you regularly exchange and who holds you accountable

2.  Form a small group that meets regularly to practice self-care or exchange experiences

3.  Look for online communities that deal with self-care

4.  Plan joint activities that serve self-care, e.g., a walk with friends

5.  Share your experiences and successes and celebrate them together

This social dimension of self-care can be particularly valuable if you find it difficult to give yourself permission for self-care.

All these practices are tools to strengthen the central support of your House of Self-Competence. They help you to take good care of yourself and thus create the basis for a stable, fulfilled life.

Remember: Self-care is not a one-time task, but a continuous process. As with a real house, this support must also be regularly checked and reinforced if necessary. With the exercises in this chapter, you have the necessary tools at hand.

In the next chapter, we will deal with the roof of our house: self-esteem, with its three aspects self-love, self-assurance, and self-confidence. This roof protects the entire house—but it can only be as stable as the foundation and the supporting walls on which it rests.

# CHAPTER 5

# The Roof - Self-Esteem

---

*"Your self-esteem is non-negotiable."*

---

## Self-Check: How's Your Self-Esteem?

Before we dive into this important chapter, take a moment for an honest self-assessment. The following characteristics indicate healthy self-esteem. How many apply to you?

- You know that you are valuable and treat yourself with love

- Your inner strength and composure radiates outward

- You don't place others' needs above your own

- You remain centered even in difficult situations

- You can accept compliments without deflecting or downplaying them

The more statements you can answer with a clear "Yes," the more stable your roof already is. But don't worry if you hesitate on some or all of these points—that's what this chapter is for.

## Understanding the Three Aspects of Self-Esteem

Self-esteem, like self-love, is a term frequently used in therapeutic contexts. "You should work on your self-esteem" or "Learn to love yourself"—we often hear such well-intentioned advice. And those affected might think: "I'd love to. But how?"

This is precisely the problem: It's impossible to consider self-esteem in isolation (without the other elements of self-competence). And it's simply impossible to work directly on self-esteem—even though numerous books claim exactly that.

If you want to strengthen your self-esteem, you must first address self-awareness, self-acceptance, self-empowerment, and self-care. When all these elements are in balance, self-esteem emerges almost by itself.

### The Three Facets of Healthy Self-Esteem

In developing the self-competence model, self-esteem was the most challenging element. Initially, we considered self-love as a separate element, but as we continued validating our model, it became increasingly clear that healthy self-esteem consists of three sub-elements that should exist in a healthy balance with each other:

### Self-love — the inward-directed self-esteem

Self-love is the inward-directed aspect of self-esteem. It is warm, appreciative, and full of genuine affection for yourself. It shows in how you speak to yourself, how you respond to your mistakes, how you care for yourself.

Self-love doesn't mean self-absorption or narcissism. It's not an inflated ego, but a quiet, deep certainty of your own worth—independent of external successes, possessions, or recognition from others.

A person with healthy self-love treats themselves with the same kindness and forbearance they would show to a loved one. They allow themselves to make mistakes, forgive themselves, and speak to themselves internally in a friendly and encouraging way.

## Self-confidence — the inner certainty of your own strength

Self-confidence is an aspect of self-esteem that radiates both inward and outward. It's the trust you have in your own personality, your abilities, and your judgment.

Externally, self-confidence can manifest in different forms—for example, through composure, calmness, or lived resilience. Internally, it creates security through knowledge of your own abilities and the certainty that you can handle difficult situations.

A person with healthy self-confidence knows they can't do everything and don't need to know everything—but they trust that they can deal with whatever comes. They don't see challenges as threats, but as opportunities for growth.

## Self-assurance — authentic outward expression

Self-assurance, on the other hand, radiates outward—in the form of appropriate presence. This by no means refers to narcissistic self-presentation. On the contrary: it's about authenticity, about "genuineness"—and that doesn't necessarily require a loud presence.

Even (and especially) introverted people can radiate strong self-assurance. It shows in the ability to stand by your own values, convictions, and needs—even when they differ from those of others.

A person with healthy self-assurance doesn't need to constantly be the center of attention or impress others. They can listen, step back, and give others space because they are sure of their own worth and don't need constant external validation.

## The Balance of the Three Aspects

These three elements together form self-esteem—ideally in harmonious balance. If one of these aspects predominates or is too weakly developed, an imbalance arises that can manifest in various ways:

- Too much self-love without sufficient self-assurance can lead to withdrawal, where you may be good with yourself but have difficulty standing up for yourself externally.

- Too much self-assurance without corresponding self-love can lead to behavior that seems strong on the outside but is hollow inside—a facade behind which self-doubt and insecurity lurk.

- Too much self-confidence without the other aspects can lead to arrogance or risk-taking because the inner connection and external corrective are missing.

The art lies in developing and nurturing all three aspects equally—like a roof that must be evenly supported on all sides to provide real protection.

## How the Roof Is Supported by All Other Elements

The image of self-esteem as a "protective roof" is apt in many ways. Just as a house roof protects against external weather influences, self-esteem also protects. If we are criticized, for instance, good self-esteem helps ensure that the criticism doesn't affect us as a person, allowing us to deal with it objectively.

Anyone who has ever been in a relationship with a narcissist knows the various and manipulative ways they can belittle others. This can go so far that the affected person's self-esteem is completely destroyed. But it's like with a house: If a severe storm removes the roof, what matters is how stable the foundation and walls are. If they're reasonably intact, the house can be repaired relatively easily. If they're not, the repair is significantly more involved.

No one would think of starting house construction with the roof. It needs a solid foundation, strong supporting walls, and a stable pillar. Only then can the roof find support.

### The Supporting Role of the Foundation

Self-esteem can only be as stable as the self-awareness on which it rests. Only when you perceive yourself clearly and undistorted—with your strengths and weaknesses, your needs and desires, your values and convictions—can healthy self-esteem develop.

Without good self-awareness, you build your self-esteem on sand—it may hold for a while, but it collapses with the first shock. With clear self-awareness, however, you have a solid foundation on which your self-esteem can rest securely.

## The Influence of the Supporting Walls

Self-acceptance is like the first supporting wall that supports your self-esteem. Only when you fully accept yourself—with all your facets, your history, your strengths and weaknesses—can true self-love emerge.

Without self-acceptance, your self-esteem remains conditional and fragile: "I am only lovable if..." or "I am only valuable if..." With healthy self-acceptance, however, you recognize your worth as a given—independent of external factors or achievements.

Self-empowerment—the second supporting wall—supports your self-esteem by giving you the experience that you can shape your life. This experience of self-efficacy is an important source of self-confidence.

Without self-empowerment, you feel helpless and powerless—an attitude that undermines your self-esteem. With healthy self-empowerment, however, you recognize yourself as an active shaper of your life, which strengthens your self-confidence and thus your self-esteem.

## The Stabilizing Effect of the Pillar

Self-care stabilizes your self-esteem by daily conveying the message: "I am worth being cared for." This continuous affirmation of your worth is an important breeding ground for self-love.

Without self-care, you send yourself the opposite message: "I am not worth being cared for." This message undermines your self-esteem insidiously but permanently. With healthy self-care, however, you daily affirm your worth, which steadily strengthens your self-esteem.

## The Harmonious Interplay

Just as a roof only offers real protection when it is evenly supported on all sides, your self-esteem can only fully develop its protective function when all elements of self-competence are well developed and work harmoniously together.

A shaky foundation, a brittle wall, or a weak support make the whole house unstable—and the roof is usually the first part to be damaged in a storm. Similarly, self-esteem is often the first element of self-competence to come under pressure when the other elements are not stable.

That's why it's so important to work on all elements of self-competence—not just self-esteem alone. Only a holistic approach can lead to stable, healthy self-esteem.

# Recognizing Typical Self-Esteem Traps

On the path to healthy self-esteem, numerous traps lurk that can lead us astray. Some come from outside, others from within—and often they reinforce each other. Here are the most common traps and how you can recognize them.

## External Threats to Self-Esteem

From the outside, self-esteem can be impaired by harsh criticism, devaluation, or manipulation. Particularly toxic are relationships with narcissistic personalities who systematically undermine their counterpart's self-esteem to exercise power and control.

A generally devaluing environment—be it in the family, at the workplace, or among friends—can also damage self-esteem in the long term. If you are constantly criticized, devalued, or ignored, this external evaluation settles in your interior over time.

The good news is: Your self-esteem can usually recover well from these external attacks if the other elements of your self-competence are intact. Like a roof that can be repaired after a storm, as long as the basic structure of the house is stable.

## The Under-Foundation Trap: Problems with Self-Awareness

More serious than external attacks are impairments that stem from problems in the other elements of self-competence. Here, the cause must be addressed first before addressing self-esteem. (If a supporting wall is at risk of collapse, it makes little sense to repair the roof first.)

If self-awareness is disturbed or only weakly developed, it's impossible to develop healthy self-esteem at all. How can you appreciate something that you don't perceive (or that you perceive only in a distorted way)?

This trap shows itself in statements like "I don't even know who I really am" or "I can't say what I actually want." Without a clear picture of yourself, your self-esteem lacks the foundation—like a roof hovering over a foggy abyss, without a foundation underneath.

## The First Wall Trap: Problems with Self-Acceptance

If you don't fully accept yourself, healthy self-esteem cannot develop either. If you struggle with your weaknesses or with decisions from the past, no appreciation or even love can grow from that. And of course, you will then radiate neither inward nor outward self-confidence.

This trap shows itself in statements like "When I finally... (am thinner, more successful, more intelligent, etc.), then I will like myself" or "I cannot forgive myself for..." Self-esteem is tied here to conditions that are either unattainable or lie in the past—both make healthy self-esteem impossible.

## The Second Wall Trap: Problems with Self-Empowerment

Let's assume your self-awareness is well developed, as is your self-acceptance—but you fail to stand up for yourself and take responsibility. Healthy self-esteem cannot emerge from this either.

If you only theoretically know what would be good for you, but don't put it into practice, this creates neither self-confidence nor does it demonstrate self-love. You simply don't value yourself enough to follow through...

This trap shows itself in statements like "I know I should actually... but somehow I never manage it" or "The others just don't let me..." Self-esteem remains stuck in the subjunctive here—a theoretical construct that is never put into reality.

## The Pillar Trap: Problems with Self-Care

Admittedly, it might work for a while even without self-care. But not in the long run. Those who don't consider themselves worth the time for themselves will not achieve self-esteem (let alone self-love).

Because self-care and self-esteem condition each other in both directions: Because you value yourself, you practice self-care. And by practicing self-care, you signal that you value yourself.

This trap shows itself in statements like "There's just no time for me" or "The others need me." Self-esteem is systematically hollowed out here by always putting yourself last.

## The Imbalance Trap: Problems with Balance

A more subtle trap is the imbalance between the three aspects of self-esteem. If one of these aspects is too strongly or too weakly developed, no harmonious self-esteem emerges:

- **Self-love without self-assurance and self-confidence**: You may be at peace with yourself, but unable to stand up for yourself externally or to take on challenges. This trap shows itself in statements like "I'm okay as I am, but I just can't..."

- **Self-assurance without self-love and self-confidence**: You appear self-assured externally, but internally you feel empty or insecure. This trap shows itself in statements like "Others think I'm super confident, but if they knew..."

- **Self-confidence without self-love and self-assurance**: You trust your abilities, but you don't really like yourself and can't appear authentically externally. This trap shows itself in statements like "I know I can do this, but somehow I still don't feel good..."

Healthy self-esteem needs all three aspects in balanced equilibrium—like a roof that must be evenly supported on all sides.

## Factors for Healthy Self-Esteem

As numerous as the obstacles and traps on the way to healthy self-esteem may be—there are just as many factors that can promote it. Here are the most important ones:

### Appreciative Upbringing and Early Imprinting

Stable self-esteem begins in childhood. Children who experience unconditional love and appreciation, who are encouraged in their strengths and accepted in their weaknesses, usually develop healthy self-esteem.

This early imprinting creates an internal image of oneself as lovable and valuable—a fundamental conviction that can withstand later challenges.

But even if your childhood was not characterized by such appreciation, it's never too late to strengthen your self-esteem. Just as a house can be renovated, your "inner house" can be rebuilt and strengthened—it just takes more awareness and effort.

### Authenticity and Self-Loyalty

Another important factor for healthy self-esteem is authenticity—the ability to stand by yourself, even if that means swimming against the current or not meeting expectations.

If you deny yourself to please others or avoid conflicts, you undermine your self-esteem in the long term. If, however, you stand by yourself, even when it's uncomfortable, you strengthen your self-assurance and thus your self-esteem.

Authenticity doesn't mean being inconsiderate or selfish. It means knowing and respecting your values, needs, and boundaries—and allowing others to do the same.

## An Appreciative Environment

Your social environment has a great influence on your self-esteem. People who appreciate you, see your strengths and accept your weaknesses, who encourage and support you—they are like additional supports for your roof.

Conversely, toxic relationships, constant criticism, or lack of appreciation can permanently weaken your self-esteem. It is therefore worthwhile to consciously pay attention to your environment and, where possible, to cultivate relationships that strengthen your self-esteem and reduce those that undermine it.

## Experience of Success and Competence

Nothing strengthens self-esteem as much as the experience of being able to do something and make a difference. Every success, every challenge mastered, every fear overcome strengthens your self-confidence and thus your self-esteem.

These don't have to be big, spectacular successes. Often it's the small, everyday experiences of self-efficacy that together make the biggest difference.

What's important is that you consciously acknowledge these successes and attribute them to yourself—instead of attributing them to chance or other factors.

## Self-Compassion and Inner Friendliness

An often overlooked but enormously important factor for healthy self-esteem is self-compassion—the ability to treat yourself kindly and understandingly, especially in difficult times or after failures.

Self-compassion means seeing yourself with the same eyes with which you would see a good friend—with understanding, patience, and the desire to help and support, rather than condemn.

This inner attitude of friendliness is the breeding ground on which self-love and thus healthy self-esteem can grow.

## Gratitude and Appreciation

Gratitude can also strengthen your self-esteem—not only gratitude for what you have or experience, but also gratitude for yourself, for your body, your mind, your abilities, and qualities.

This attitude of appreciation directs the gaze to what is (instead of what is missing) and thus creates a feeling of abundance and being enough—important foundations for healthy self-esteem.

# Practical Steps to More Self-Esteem, Self-Love, and Self-Confidence

Theory is important—but only practical implementation brings real change. Here you'll find concrete exercises that will help you strengthen your self-esteem. Choose the ones that appeal to you and integrate them into your daily life.

## Exercise 1: The Self-Esteem Journal

This exercise helps you sharpen your awareness of your strengths and positive qualities, thus strengthening your self-love.

Here's how:

1. Take a nice notebook that is only intended for this purpose

2. Every evening, note three things you did well that day—no matter how small they may seem

3. Additionally, note one quality or ability that you appreciate about yourself

4. Regularly read through what you've written to get a more complete picture of yourself

This exercise consciously directs your attention to your strengths and successes, which we often overlook or take for granted in everyday life. Over time, a more positive, realistic self-image emerges.

## Exercise 2: Mirror of Integrity

This creative exercise helps you strengthen the connection between self-esteem and lived self-empowerment.

Here's how:

1. Once a week, consciously take time (5-10 minutes) and ask yourself: "Where did I act in accordance with my values this week—even when it was difficult?"

2. Write down 1-3 situations, even small moments.

3. Afterwards, look in a mirror (or at your own portrait) and say aloud: "I remained true to myself. That makes me valuable."

This exercise strengthens self-esteem through authenticity and inner coherence—not through achievement or external recognition.

## Exercise 3: The "What If I Were Valuable?" Question

If your self-esteem happens to be unstable, this exercise serves to playfully dissolve inner blockades through a paradoxical perspective.

Here's how:

1. In the morning or before challenging situations, ask yourself the following question: "What would I think, feel, or do differently today if I knew deep down that I am completely valuable?"

2. Spontaneously note 2-3 answers—without having to implement them.

This hypothetical form bypasses critical defense mechanisms and makes new, self-esteem-strengthening scopes of action visible.

## Exercise 4: Success Visualization

This exercise strengthens your self-confidence by helping you remember your successes and strengths and recall them in difficult situations.

Here's how:

1. Remember three situations in which you were particularly successful or competent—moments you are proud of

2. Visualize each of these situations as vividly as possible: What did you see, hear, feel? What was your posture? What were you thinking?

3. Find a symbol or a word for each of these success memories that reminds you of them

4. Recall this symbol or word before challenging situations to remind yourself of your strength and competence

This technique uses the power of memory and imagination to strengthen your self-confidence in difficult moments. It's as if you're taking the power of your successes with you into new challenges.

## Exercise 5: Compliment Acceptance

This exercise helps you strengthen your self-esteem by teaching you to accept positive feedback instead of deflecting it.

Here's how:

1. When someone gives you a compliment, consciously accept it instead of deflecting or downplaying it

2. Take a deep breath and simply say "Thank you"—without further explanations or relativizations

3. Feel how the compliment feels and allow yourself to enjoy it

4. Later note the compliment in your self-esteem journal to create a collection of these positive feedbacks

Many people with low self-esteem have the habit of deflecting or downplaying compliments—as if they weren't worthy of being praised. This exercise helps you break this habit and accept appreciation from outside as confirmation of your worth.

## Exercise 6: The Self-Compassion Ritual

This exercise helps you develop more self-love by teaching you to deal compassionately with yourself in difficult moments.

Here's how:

1. When you've made a mistake or feel uncomfortable, pause briefly and place a hand on your heart

2. Tell yourself internally or quietly: "This is a difficult moment. All people make mistakes and feel pain. How can I now be friendly and understanding with myself?"

3. Consider what a good friend would say to you in this situation, and say it to yourself

4. Ask yourself what you need now to feel better, and fulfill this wish as far as possible

This exercise breaks the automatism of self-criticism and replaces it with an attitude of compassion and care—an important foundation for healthy self-love.

## Exercise 7: Inner Strength Activation

This exercise strengthens your self-confidence by helping you activate your inner strength and use it in challenging situations.

Here's how:

1. Find a body posture that expresses strength and self-confidence for you (upright posture, firm stance, open shoulders, etc.)

2. Consciously adopt this posture and feel how it affects your feeling

3.  Add a gesture or a sentence that symbolizes power and strength for you

4.  Practice this combination regularly so that you can easily recall it in challenging situations

This technique uses the interaction between body and mind to strengthen your self-confidence. Through the changed body posture, you signal to your brain: "I am strong and self-assured"— and your brain responds accordingly.

All these exercises are tools to strengthen the roof of your house of self-competence. They help you develop healthy self-esteem with all three aspects—self-love, self-confidence, and self-assurance— and thus complete the crowning of your house.

Remember: Self-esteem is closely connected with all other elements of self-competence. If you have difficulties with your self-esteem, it's worth taking a look at the other elements as well—the foundation of self-awareness, the supporting walls of self-acceptance and self-empowerment, and the supporting pillar of self-care.

Healthy self-esteem doesn't emerge overnight, nor through a few affirmations or exercises. It grows organically from the totality of your self-competence. But with each step you take on this path, your "house" becomes more stable, safer, and more comfortable—a place where you feel good and at home, whatever life may bring.

In the next chapter, we will look at how all elements of the house work together and how you can nurture and strengthen your personal house of self-competence as a whole.

CHAPTER 6

# The Whole House - Integration

---

*"The whole is more than the sum of its parts."*

- **Aristotle**

---

In the preceding chapters, we've gotten to know the individual elements of the house of self-competence: the foundation of self-awareness, the supporting walls of self-acceptance and self-empowerment, the supporting pillar of self-care, and the protective roof of self-esteem.

But as with a real house, it's not enough to understand the individual components—what matters is how they work together and form a harmonious whole. In this chapter, we will therefore take a step back and look at the entire house of self-competence.

## How the Elements Work Together

The house of self-competence is not a static structure but a living system in which all elements are in relationship with each other and influence each other. Each element supports and strengthens the others—and conversely is supported and strengthened by them.

## The Upward Spiral of Self-Competence

When you work on one element, it positively affects all the others. This positive feedback can set an upward spiral in motion:

- Improved **self-awareness** allows you to see yourself more clearly and thus accept yourself more easily. It helps you recognize what you can and should take responsibility for. It shows you what you need to take good care of yourself. And it gives you a clearer picture of your worth.

- Stronger **self-acceptance** allows you to perceive more openly and honestly, without going into defense. It gives you the security to take responsibility, even when not everything runs perfectly. It creates space for loving self-care. And it nourishes unconditional self-esteem.

- More pronounced **self-empowerment** sharpens your perception of your room for maneuver. It lets you recognize that you can accept yourself as you are and at the same time work on yourself. It motivates you to actively care for yourself. And it strengthens your self-confidence and thus your self-esteem.

- Better **self-care** refines your self-awareness by bringing you in contact with your needs. It gives you the energy to work on your self-acceptance. It creates the space you need to take responsibility. And it sends you the daily message: "You are worth it"—the basis of healthy self-esteem.

- Stronger **self-esteem** in turn gives you the security to perceive honestly and clearly, without judging yourself. It makes self-acceptance easier for you because you know your fundamental worth. It encourages you to take responsibility because you believe in your abilities. And it motivates you to take good care of yourself because you know you deserve it.

These interactions show how each element strengthens all others and is strengthened by them. This also means: No matter which element you work on—you always strengthen the entire house.

## Recognizing and Breaking the Downward Spiral

Unfortunately, this interaction also works in the other direction. When one element is weakened, it can trigger a downward spiral that destabilizes the entire house:

- Distorted **self-awareness** makes self-acceptance difficult because you have a distorted image of yourself. It hinders your self-empowerment because you don't clearly recognize your room for maneuver. It complicates self-care because you don't perceive your needs. And it undermines your self-esteem because your self-image is distorted.

- Lacking **self-acceptance** leads to defense mechanisms that cloud your self-awareness. It prevents you from taking full responsibility because you're afraid of mistakes. It blocks loving self-care because you don't think you deserve it. And it makes healthy self-esteem impossible because you don't fully accept yourself.

This pattern continues for all elements. The good news is: You can break this downward spiral at any point by consciously working on one element. Often it's easiest to start with the element that seems most accessible to you—be it self-awareness, self-acceptance, self-empowerment, or self-care.

As soon as you make initial progress there, the other elements will also begin to improve, and the downward spiral slowly transforms into an upward spiral.

## Typical Development Paths

Every person has their own story, their own strengths and challenges. Accordingly, there are also many different ways in which the house of self-competence can develop. Nevertheless, some typical patterns can be identified.

### The Holistic Construction

Ideally, self-competence develops organically and balanced, like a house that is built by experienced master builders: First, a solid foundation of self-awareness is laid. On top of that, the supporting walls of self-acceptance and self-empowerment are erected. The supporting pillar of self-care stabilizes the building. And finally, the protective roof of self-esteem is put on.

This ideal-typical development path is particularly promoted by a loving, appreciative upbringing. Children who are perceived in their needs and feelings, who are accepted as they are, who are allowed to take age-appropriate responsibility, whose self-care is supported, and whose worth is confirmed—they often develop a stable, balanced house of self-competence.

But this ideal development path is rare. Most of us experience challenges throughout our lives that weaken or strengthen certain elements of our house and thus lead to uneven developments.

## The Intellectual Path

Some people build their house of self-competence primarily through the intellect. They develop good intellectual self-awareness and self-reflection. They understand cognitively that self-acceptance is important, and willingly take self-empowerment. Perhaps they even systematically plan their self-care.

But emotionally, the house often remains somewhat cool and uninhabited. The "rational architecture" is impressive, but it lacks the emotional warmth of lived self-acceptance, the lightness of intuitive self-care, and the deep anchoring of self-esteem in feeling.

For people on this development path, it can be helpful to engage more with their feelings and their body, for example through mindfulness exercises, creative forms of expression, or body-oriented practices.

## The Emotional Path

Other people build their house primarily through feeling. They have good access to their emotions and their body and are often empathetic and sensitive. They may have developed intuitive self-care and can emotionally accept themselves well.

But self-empowerment and cognitive self-reflection are perhaps less pronounced. The house is warm and cozy, but structurally not always stable. It lacks the clear architecture of conscious self-awareness and the supporting framework of self-empowerment.

For people on this development path, it can be helpful to bring more awareness and structure into their house, for example through systematic self-reflection, clear goals and boundaries, or conscious decision-making processes.

## The Detour via Achievement

Many people in our achievement-oriented society try to build their house of self-competence via the detour of achievement and external recognition. They believe that they are only valuable when they achieve something special, and try to "earn" their self-esteem.

This path often leads to an unstable house: The self-esteem is dependent on external confirmation, the self-acceptance is tied to conditions, the self-awareness is fixated on success and failure, and self-care is neglected in favor of more and more achievement.

For people on this development path, it can be a liberating realization that their worth does not depend on their achievements, but is inherent to them as human beings. The path here often leads through deeper self-awareness and more unconditional self-acceptance.

## The Path Through Crisis

Sometimes it takes a crisis for us to deal with our self-competence. An exhaustive depression, a failed relationship, a professional failure, or a life crisis can force us to pause and look at our "house."

In such crises, it often becomes clear which elements of our house are particularly unstable—perhaps we have neglected self-awareness, tied self-acceptance to conditions, avoided self-empowerment, or forgotten self-care.

As painful as crises may be, they offer an opportunity for profound change and growth. They can be the starting point to consciously work on your own self-competence and build a more stable, more authentic house.

## When an Element Falters – Repair Work on the House

Just like a real house, the house of self-competence can suffer damage or develop weak spots. Sometimes a certain element is particularly affected and needs special attention.

### When the Foundation Wobbles: Work on Self-Awareness

Signs of an unstable foundation of self-awareness can be:

- You often feel disoriented or "beside yourself"
- You don't know what you really want or need
- You are repeatedly surprised by your own reactions
- You have the impression that you don't really know yourself

If you notice such signs in yourself, it makes sense to consciously work on your self-awareness:

- Take regular time for self-reflection, for example through journaling or meditation
- Consciously pay attention to your body sensations, thoughts, and feelings in everyday life
- Ask trusted people for honest feedback on how they perceive you

- If necessary, work with a coach or therapist to recognize blind spots

Remember: When the foundation becomes more stable, all other elements of your house benefit from it.

## When the First Wall Crumbles: Work on Self-Acceptance

Signs of an unstable wall of self-acceptance can be:

- You are very self-critical and hard on yourself
- You constantly compare yourself with others and feel inadequate
- You struggle with your past and cannot forgive yourself
- You only feel valuable when you fulfill certain conditions

If you notice such signs in yourself, it makes sense to consciously work on your self-acceptance:

- Practice self-compassion and a friendly inner voice
- Recognize that mistakes and weaknesses are part of being human
- Work on forgiveness for past decisions
- Free yourself from excessive or perfectionist demands

Remember: When this supporting wall becomes stronger, it better carries all other elements of your house.

## When the Second Wall Falters: Work on Self-Empowerment

Signs of an unstable wall of self-empowerment can be:

- You often feel like a victim of circumstances or other people
- You postpone decisions or avoid them altogether

- You blame others when something doesn't work out
- You have the feeling that you have no influence on your life

If you notice such signs in yourself, it makes sense to consciously work on your self-empowerment:

- Practice making conscious decisions, even in small matters
- Pay attention to your language: Replace "I must" or "I should" with "I decide to"
- Focus on what you can influence, instead of on what is outside your control
- Set yourself small, achievable goals and celebrate your successes

Remember: When this supporting wall becomes stronger, it gives more support to all other elements of your house.

## When the Support Gives Way: Work on Self-Care

Signs of an unstable support of self-care can be:

- You feel chronically exhausted or burned out
- You neglect your basic needs such as sleep, nutrition, or exercise
- You can't set boundaries well and say "no"
- You have the feeling of constantly being there for others, but never for yourself

If you notice such signs in yourself, it makes sense to consciously work on your self-care:

- Make self-care a priority and consciously plan it into your everyday life

- Identify what personally does you good and gives you energy
- Practice setting boundaries and saying "no" when something becomes too much
- Develop healthy routines for sleep, nutrition, exercise, and relaxation

Remember: When this support becomes stronger, it stabilizes the entire house of your self-competence.

## When the Roof Leaks: Work on Self-Esteem

Signs of an unstable roof of self-esteem can be:

- You often feel inferior or "not good enough"
- You are strongly dependent on the recognition and confirmation of others
- You cannot accept compliments or don't believe them
- You have the feeling that you constantly have to prove yourself

If you notice such signs in yourself, it's important to understand that self-esteem builds on all other elements. Therefore, it can be helpful to first check which other elements might need special attention.

In addition, you can strengthen your self-esteem:

- Practice acknowledging and appreciating your successes and strengths
- Treat yourself with the same kindness and appreciation that you would show to a good friend

- Learn to accept compliments without deflecting or downplaying them
- Regularly remind yourself of your inherent worth as a human being, independent of achievements or external confirmation

Remember: A stable roof protects the entire house of your self-competence from the "weather influences" of life.

## Long-term Care of Your House of Self-Competence

A house needs not only one-time construction work or occasional repairs—it also needs continuous care and attention to remain inhabitable and cozy in the long term. The same applies to your house of self-competence.

### Regular Inspections: Self-Reflection as a Habit

Just as a wise homeowner regularly inspects his house to detect damage early, it is helpful to regularly look at your house of self-competence:

- Take regular time for conscious self-reflection, for example weekly or monthly
- Ask yourself questions like: How is my self-awareness? How accepting am I with myself? How well do I take responsibility for my life? How well do I care for myself? How does my self-esteem feel?
- Pay special attention to areas that might need attention

- Also celebrate the progress and strengths that you observe in yourself

This regular self-reflection helps you to recognize small problems early and address them before they become bigger difficulties.

## Preventive Measures: Living Self-Competence in Everyday Life

Just as a homeowner takes preventive measures to protect his house from damage, you can also work preventively on your self-competence:

- Integrate the exercises from the previous chapters into your everyday life so that they become a habit
- Pay attention to warning signals such as persistent stress, exhaustion, or emotional strain and respond to them early
- Surround yourself with people who strengthen your self-competence instead of undermining it
- Create routines and structures that support your self-competence, e.g., regular times for self-care or reflection

These preventive measures continuously strengthen your house of self-competence and make it more resistant to the challenges of life.

## Dealing with Storms: Resilience in Times of Crisis

No matter how strong your house may be—sometimes storms come up that can shake it. Life crises, losses, illnesses, or other severe burdens can put your self-competence to the test.

In such times, it's important to take especially good care of your house:

- Focus on the most fundamental elements: clear self-awareness and gentle self-care

- Be especially friendly and compassionate with yourself

- Remember that crises pass and that your house has weathered previous storms as well

- Don't hesitate to seek professional help if you feel that the burden is becoming too great

With a well-maintained house of self-competence, you can weather even severe storms—perhaps with some damage that needs to be repaired, but the foundation and supporting structures remain intact.

## The Lifelong Construction Site: Growth and Development

A house of self-competence is never "finished"—it's a lifelong construction site that continuously develops and grows. This is not a burden, but a gift: The possibility to find more and more to yourself, to get to know yourself more deeply, to accept yourself more completely, to take responsibility more consciously, to care for yourself more lovingly, and to feel your worth more deeply.

It's not about perfection. It's about creating a house where you feel comfortable, where you can be who you really are, and from which you can enter into relationship with others and the world.

Such a house is a gift—not only to yourself but also to everyone who comes into contact with you. Because the more stable and authentic your house of self-competence is, the more you can also be a safe, supportive place for other people.

With this chapter, the circle of our journey through the house of self-competence closes. We have explored the foundation of self-awareness, looked at the supporting walls of self-acceptance and self-empowerment, gotten to know the supporting pillar of self-care, and understood the protective roof of self-esteem. Now it's up to you to use this knowledge to build, maintain, and enjoy your own house of self-competence—a house that gives you security, freedom, and vitality, whatever life may bring.

# The Authors

**Susanne Salig** is a holistic psychotherapist, certified coach, and compassionate guide for women in times of personal transition. With deep intuition, warmth, and many years of experience, she helps individuals release old patterns, reconnect with themselves, and access their inner strength. As a co-developer of the Self-Competence Model, she draws on a rich background in advanced methods such as clinical hypnosis, EMDR, and hypnosystemic therapy. In both her practice and her programs, she places the uniqueness and depth of each human being at the center.

**Arne Salig** is a psychological counselor with over 25 years of experience and a recognized expert in self-competence, resilience, and personal transformation. Together with his wife Susanne and psychologist Melanie Theissler, he developed the Self-Competence Model, which is now applied in therapy, coaching, and leadership development. His work bridges deep psychological insight with practical tools for everyday life—always aiming to help people find greater inner strength and clarity. In addition to his psychological work, he also advises organizations on quality management and people-centered leadership.

**www.self-competence.org**

# Your Personal
# Self-Competence Check-Out

What is the single most important insight you gained from this book?

Which part of your House of Self-Competence needs the most attention right now?

What part of yourself do you understand better now?

What is one self-commitment you want to make for the next seven days?

How will you integrate these insights into your everyday life – starting today?

# Do you want to go deeper?

This book is a beginning –
but your journey doesn't have to end here.
If you're ready to integrate what you've discovered,
break through old patterns, and unlock your next level
of inner growth, we invite you to explore more at:

www.self-competence.com

The Self-Code
A 7-week online course to build your inner house step by step.
Practical. Clear. Empowering.

Mentoring with Arne Salig
6 months. Deep growth. True inner leadership.
For individuals who are ready for real transformation.

VIP Day
One day. One decision. A new level of clarity.
High-impact coaching at exclusive locations in Europe.

**ARNE SALIG**
SELF-COMPETENCE

Whatever your path – we're here to support your next step.
Self-competence is not just a concept. It's a way of living.

www.ingramcontent.com/pod-product-compliance
Lightning Source LLC
Chambersburg PA
CBHW051632120626
46551CB00014B/2037